PHILOSOPHICAL CLASSICS

General Editor : G. H. R. PARKINSON

KANT

PROLEGOMENA

IMMANUEL KANT

PROLEGOMENA

TO ANY

FUTURE METAPHYSICS

THAT WILL BE ABLE TO PRESENT ITSELF

AS A SCIENCE

A TRANSLATION FROM THE GERMAN
BASED ON THE ORIGINAL EDITIONS
WITH AN INTRODUCTION AND NOTES

by

PETER G. LUCAS

MANCHESTER UNIVERSITY PRESS

Published by the
University of Manchester
at the
UNIVERSITY PRESS
316–324 *Oxford Road, Manchester* M13 9NR

First published 1953
Second impression 1959
Third impression 1962
Reprinted 1966
Reprinted 1971

ISBN 0 7190 0492 6

Printed in Great Britain by
Butler & Tanner Ltd, Frome and London

TABLE OF CONTENTS

PROLEGOMENA

TO ANY FUTURE METAPHYSICS THAT WILL BE ABLE TO PRESENT ITSELF AS A SCIENCE

Table compiled from headings in the text. The original editions have no tables of Contents

TRANSLATOR'S PREFACE

THE *Critique of Pure Reason* is not the dyad that it is commonly taken to be, but a triad. In addition to the two editions of 1781 and 1787 there are the *Prolegomena*—Kant's own guide, as he called it, to the first edition and the source of some of the changes in the second edition. For the present-day reader they have a twofold value. They were written (we follow Kant in using the plural) to provide a short survey of the main points in the *Critique* which would make it less difficult to understand. To enable them to serve this purpose again is perhaps the main justification for this new version.

The book was not however to be a mere summary or simplification of the *Critique*—which would be quite out of character for Kant—but an approach to the subject by a new method, which he called 'analytic' in contrast to the 'synthetic method' of the *Critique*. It was to gain its simplicity by starting from the known and proceeding to the unknown. The existence and universal validity of mathematics and natural science, and of metaphysics 'as a natural disposition', are taken for granted, thereby avoiding a large quantity of argument that was needed in the *Critique*, and on this basis the 'possibility' of mathematics, natural science and a future scientific metaphysics is shown. But Kant seems to have seen subsequently that this kind of exposition had a place to fill in the *Critique* itself. In the Second Edition he incorporated matter from the *Prolegomena* (in part verbatim), including the formula 'how are synthetic *a priori* judgements possible?' which is given a leading position for the first time in the *Prolegomena*. The significance of these additions to the *Critique* in Kant's philosophy as a whole will be apparent to the reader who has seen them in their original setting and appreciated there the significance of the 'analytic' method.

This may be counted the sixth or seventh version to be published in English, though the last two were revisions going back to Mahaffy's versions of 1872 and 1889. This is a completely new translation based on the original editions. It is intended to be as authentic a reproduction of what Kant published as the circumstances of translation permit. Through the application of certain principles, stated in the Introduction, and the exercise of meticulous care, we believe that the degree of authenticity that can be reached is much higher than has been assumed in the past.

It is the first translation to have put right as fully as is possible the confusion that arose in parts of the original text through some series of mishaps during the printing (and is reproduced without comment in the Academy edition and all the previous translations except the latest).

I have received generous assistance from many quarters. In addition to the valuable help given by my colleagues in Manchester and elsewhere, I have to record with gratitude a linguistic revision of the translation by Mr. J. P. Stern in Cambridge and a philosophical revision of the Introduction and text by Mr. W. H. Walsh in Oxford, whose assistance in removing numerous errors and obscurities makes them in no way responsible for those that remain.

INTRODUCTION

ORIGIN OF THE PROLEGOMENA

The *Critique of Pure Reason* was published in the early summer of 1781, the *Prolegomena* about Easter, 1783. Kant expected the *Critique* to have a revolutionary effect and anxiously awaited its impact on the world of learning. In fact he found that it was being received in silence (p. 151). It was first reviewed on 19th January 1782 (p. 143) in a tone which was at best non-committal, and not again until 24th August 1782 (p. 151), and he heard privately from friends that his book was being found obscure and unintelligible, and put aside as unreadable (p. 10).

The *Prolegomena* were the fruit of Kant's intention to rectify this state of affairs. There is mention of such an intention in a letter from Kant to M. Herz as early as 11th May 1781, but the history of the composition of the *Prolegomena* between this date and 1783 is not clear. From August 1781 onwards there are allusions in letters from Hamann to a forthcoming book by Kant, and these can be read as suggesting, although quite inconclusively, that Kant may have had two distinct plans : a popular work, to introduce his philosophy to laymen, and an abstract of or supplement to the *Critique* for the expert. All that can be said with any confidence is that in the second half of 1781 Kant was definitely intending to publish and probably working on a short book intended to make the *Critique* more accessible. His reaction to the Göttingen review of January 1782 was incorporated into this book, both indirectly in the body of the book and directly in a full reply at the end. The book was finished in the autumn of 1782—Kant has 'just now' seen the Gotha review of August 1782 (p. 151)—and after unexpected delay with the printer, published about Easter, 1783. The relevant documents for this brief history are collected in the notes to the Prussian Academy edition of the collected works. Any further information about its composition must be drawn from internal evidence, in particular from comparison with the *Critique*.

BASIS OF THE TEXT

The translation has been made from copies of two of the original editions. There are at least five typographically distinguishable versions all bearing the date 1783, which have been described in the notes to the Academy edition. The textual differences between them are of the most trivial kind, and as there were no further authorised editions in Kant's lifetime, no question of variant readings arises.

The question of emendations is only a little more difficult. K. Vorländer's text of the *Prolegomena*, 6th edition, 1920 (*Philosophische Bibliothek*), assembles all proposed emendations to the text, including some that are unnecessary. Those that are beyond doubt (corrections of misprints and some obvious errors—' objective ' for ' subjective ', ' reason ' for ' nature ', ' material ' for ' immaterial ', etc.) have been silently incorporated and the few mistakes in Vorländer's own text put right. Those that are plausible but not beyond doubt have been recorded only in footnotes, together with a few new emendations proposed by the translator.

In the original editions (and in all previous translations except the most recent) there is considerable confusion in § 2 and § 4, part of which appears to be the result of the third and fourth galleys having been accidentally transposed, so that some paragraphs belonging to the end of § 2 appear in the middle of § 4. The facts are that in the original editions § 4 contains a passage (pp. 21 to 24 in this translation) which first aroused comment in 1879 as incongruous, but which follows with no incongruity if placed at the end of § 2 as printed. The source of the error is clear from the fact that in print the passage is exactly 100 lines long, occupies lines 301–400 of the text as printed, and in its correct position would occupy lines 201–300. The Academy edition makes no mention of this manifest error.

A further fault in the same passage may be conjectured. The context seems to demand a paragraph on natural science, but no such paragraph appears. When Kant copied parts of § 2 into the expanded introduction to the second edition of the *Critique,* he broke off where § 2 breaks off as printed and continued with a newly written passage which contains both the gist of the part of § 2 that was 'lost' in § 4 and a short paragraph on natural science. We have incorporated this latter paragraph (p. 22) from the *Critique,* though the passage on natural science which we believe to have been lost from the *Prolegomena* would have been longer, to be in balance with the rest of § 2. Full details are given in footnotes.

Yet a further fault in § 2—a paragraph (p. 20) clearly intended to be a parenthesis or footnote, which has found its way into the body of the text—has been adjusted by means of a footnote.

PRINCIPLES OF TRANSLATION

The primary aim of this translation is to present an English version corresponding with the strictest achievable philological as well as philosophical authenticity to what Kant wrote, so that any philosophically significant analysis of the English text, of the form of expression as well as of the substance, and of detail as well as of the general plan, should yield results as nearly as possible the same as those of a similar analysis of the German text. The voice that is heard speaking in these pages is intended to sound like the voice of Kant and not like that of a twentieth-century academic philosopher. The final justification claimed for this method, apart from its conformity to standards of scholarship, is that it makes Kant more easily intelligible, not less easily, than if his words are disguised in modern dress.

In particular, the following principles have been applied as far as seemed consistent with common sense.

Internal consistency : As far as possible a given German word (unless it is one with several meanings evidently separate for Kant) has been rendered by the same English word ; that is to say supposed English usage and the influence of context have been given much less weight than is customary. The reasons for this are that assessment of contextual influences is found in practice to be a highly personal matter which can let in a flood of private interpretations, and ' usage ' is strongly local and ephemeral. A text of this standing may be allowed, within reason, to create its own usage, and in any case Kant's German is often a good deal stranger than the passages of somewhat unusual English which will be found here. Further and more important, one of the soundest ways for a student of Kant to learn the meaning of any given term is to observe how and in what contexts it occurs, which he is prevented from doing if the translator has already altered the word to suit the context.

Metaphors and images : Great care has been exercised to keep as far as possible the same pictures in words with a metaphorical or quasi-metaphorical use and in abstract words which include etymologically a concrete root, and particularly not to introduce any non-Kantian images. Thus for instance Kant writes of past philosophy mainly in terms of walking along a road and of future philosophy in terms of taking aim at a target set up, as in shooting practice, at not too great a distance. Kant's thought can be falsified by using the words ' development ' and ' purpose ' respectively in these circumstances, which would perhaps be the most ' ordinary ' usage in present-day English.

Punctuation etc. : Quotation marks, heavy type (represented here by italics), and indention have been reproduced exactly as in the original editions. Consistency in this respect implied that the colon should also be retained in most instances, even though it conflicts with English usage, since Kant uses it in some cases in the same way as these devices. They are all used sometimes merely for emphasis and sometimes to mark off a sentence in a way that has some affinity with the current distinction between mention and use. Kant's abbreviations have also been retained.

Sentence construction : All Kant's translators become obsessed with the tremendous length of his sentences. In so far as this is merely a question of his not using a full stop where one is possible, these sentences can be broken up with nothing but profit. But there is another kind of very long sentence, the length of which is not a mere stylistic idiosyncrasy but is a significant consequence of Kant's philosophical method. Kant's characteristic way of thinking and his conception of reason as only corrigible from within itself (i.e. by surveying the relations of its parts) makes it part of his philosophical impulse to hold an unusually large number of ideas for consideration together and to need simultaneously a large number of qualifications and expressions of relations. It is not easy to break up such sentences without falsifying the thought by giving what is really synopsis the appearance of inference. In the translation such sentences, though sometimes still long, have been broken down as far as (and often further than) could be done without loss.

Comment and interpretation appear, not in the form of interpolation or paraphrase in the text, but strictly confined to footnotes.

Authorities : In addition to the well-known commentaries on the *Critique* and the usual linguistic works of reference, the following dictionary, being roughly contemporary with the *Prolegomena*, has been an invaluable guide : Johann Christoph Adelung : *Grammatisch-kritisches Wörterbuch der Hochdeutschen Mundart.* 2nd edition, Leipzig, 1793–1801.

INTRODUCTION

Previous Translations of the Prolegomena into English

John Richardson : Metaphysical Works of the celebrated Immanuel Kant translated from the German with a sketch of his life and writings by J. R. many years a student of the Kantian philosophy. Containing . . . 2. Prolegomena to future metaphysics. London, 1836. (*Separate title page for the Prolegomena :* London, printed for W. Simpkin and R. Marshall, 1819.[1])

John P. Mahaffy and John H. Bernard : Kant's Critical Philosophy for English Readers by J. P. M. Volume III The Prolegomena. London, Macmillan, 1872, 2nd (new and completed) edition by J. P. M. & J. H. B. Volume II 1889, 3rd edition 1915.

Ernest Belfort Bax : Kant's Prolegomena and Metaphysical Foundations of Natural Science, translated from the original by E. B. B. Bohn's Philosophical Library. London, G. Bell & Sons, 1883.

Paul Carus : Kant's Prolegomena to any future metaphysics edited in English by P. C. La Salle, Ill., Open Court Pub. Co., 1902, reprinted 1947.

Lewis White Beck : Prolegomena to any future metaphysics. Immanuel Kant. A revision of the Carus translation edited with an introduction by L. W. B. New York, The Liberal Arts Press, 1951.

In making the present translation all the above have been compared.

[1] Not 1818, as reported by Mahaffy and widely repeated.

AIDS TO STUDY

The Structure of the Prolegomena in Relation to the Critique of Pure Reason

The general relation of the *Prolegomena* to the *Critique* is that of a guide or plan (pp. 13, 152). The *Prolegomena* are not however uniform in manner, and we may distinguish two main ways in which this function is carried out :

    (i) Exposition of the material of the *Critique*, in the form of :

        (*a*) independent re-statement according to a method called by Kant ' analytic ' (pp. 13, 29, 31 n.) of what was expressed in the *Critique* ' synthetically ', including a few improvements which are taken up into the 2nd edition of the *Critique*. (The Transcendental Aesthetic and Analytic are in the main re-stated in this way.)

        (*b*) brief summary with direct reference to the *Critique*. (The Transcendental Dialectic is treated thus.)

    (ii) Explanation of Kant's estimate of contemporary philosophers and schools, in particular

        (*a*) Hume

        (*b*) dogmatic metaphysics and common sense (stated with forceful polemic).

The detailed correspondences under (i) between paragraphs of the *Prolegomena* and sections of the *Critique* are shown below in a comparative table. The material under (ii) does not correspond directly to any part of the *Critique*, though some of it is taken up into the new Preface to the second edition.

(i) The Analytic Method as guide to the Synthetic Method.

The nature of the analytic method of exposition—proceeding from the known to the unknown (p. 29)—emerges fairly clearly from a comparison of the earlier part of the *Prolegomena* with the corresponding parts of the *Critique*. The *Prolegomena* begin from established fact—the existence of mathematics, of natural science, and of the unsatisfied demand for metaphysics (which must be capable of satisfaction, because everything in nature has a useful end (p. 130))—and shows how the system of pure intuitions of the senses, categories of the understanding and ideas of reason establishes for Kant the ' possibility ' of mathematics, natural science and metaphysics ; that is to say, this epistemological system is held by Kant to make it intelligible that mathematics and natural science exist, and that metaphysics could exist, and thus also to constitute an instruction for bringing metaphysics into being. The system is not strictly speaking deduced or proved in the *Prolegomena* but is merely presented ; the successful reader will have understood the system but will not have had insight into the grounds of proof of its correctness. For this he can go to the *Critique*, where (in so far, we must add, as it is in fact synthetic in method) nothing is assumed and everything is deduced and proved from ' elements '— a deduction and proof which will now be the more lucid to him for having first understood the system as a whole.

In the third part of the ' Main Question ', on metaphysics as a natural disposition and the ideas of reason, Kant does not adhere to the distinction between analytic *Prolegomena* and a synthetic *Critique*, but follows the Transcendental Dialectic fairly closely with summaries that are always short and sometimes little more than mere mentions of sections of the Dialectic. This apparent defection from his plan may well be the unavoidable consequence of the fact that in this case he is not examining actually existing sciences, but criticising an existing pseudo-science, metaphysics.

The last main section, on how scientific metaphysics is to come into being, corresponds, in that this is its problem, to the Transcendental Doctrine of Method, but it is so brief —it asserts little more than that the *Critique* has now made it possible for the job to start—that there is nothing to say about its method of exposition.

It may be remarked in general that the analytic method brings Kant's ultimate purpose—to create a scientific metaphysics—much more prominently into the foreground than does the synthetic method of the *Critique*, and in so doing reproduces the moving force impelling Kant's philosophical endeavours more genuinely than the *Critique*. In intellectual life in general, the analytical method is the method of discovery, the synthetic method the method of proof. In reverting to the analytic method in the *Prolegomena*, Kant is returning to the processes through which he arrived at the Transcendental Philosophy, both explicitly, in a few passages where he describes the successive stages on the way to the *Critique* (pp. 9 f., 85 f.), and implicitly in the arrangement of the *Prolegomena* as a whole.

(ii) Kant's estimate of his contemporaries as a guide to the *Critique*.

Kant's account of how he partially accepted and then moved forward from Hume's position is clear and no doubt makes a contribution to the intelligibility of the discourse. The polemic against ungrounded dogmatic confidence in metaphysics on the one hand and on the other against the renunciation of metaphysics by the continental popular agnostic philosophies of probable conjecture and the Scottish philosophy of common sense, both of which lead to materialism and scepticism, serve to mark by contrast Kant's own middle way (p. 128).

It has been maintained and denied, in an acrimonious academic controversy in Berlin in 1878–80, that these passages, having no direct counterpart in the *Critique*, are additions to his first plan of an abstract of the *Critique* for experts, which Kant was prompted to make by the Göttingen review and other information that he was gathering about its reception. Each separately, the supposed abstract and the additions, are said to constitute an independent whole. After making these additions Kant would have dropped the other supposed plan for a separate popular work. B. Erdmann published an edition of the *Prolegomena* in 1878 in which what he believed to be additions were distinguished by smaller type. Apart from the few highly inconclusive allusions in the correspondence mentioned above, the hypothesis is based solely on internal evidence and therefore amounts to no more than the distinction between two types of writing that we are making here.

The list of Erdmann's supposed additions, which thus constitutes a list of the polemical passages and those lighter in tone which are not part of the main argument, is as follows : Preface, § 2 (p. 21 " I cannot refrain . . ."— p. 22 ". . . fine style "), § 3, § 4 (p. 28 " In the Critique . . ."—p. 29 ". . . analytic "), § 5 (p. 30 " But here we cannot . . ."—". . . boundaries of the same ", and p. 32 " Indispensable . . ."—p. 33 ". . . in analytic form "), Notes I–III, §§ 27–31, § 39, § 46 (foot-note), § 48 (footnote), § 49 (p. 102 " In this way . . ."—". . . Cartesian idealism "), § 57–end of the *Prolegomena*.

COMPARATIVE TABLE OF THE PROLEGOMENA AND THE CRITIQUE

The following table is a complete parallel list of the main sections of the *Critique* and the paragraphs of the *Prolegomena*. The sections and paragraphs that have the same primary intention are placed opposite each other in the table. The reader may confidently turn for elucidation from passages of either to the corresponding passage of the other. There are of course innumerable correspondences of detail, spread over the whole of the *Critique* and the *Prolegomena*, which could only be exhausted in a large index.

TABLE OF SPECIAL TERMS

An explanation of the special terms used by Kant is to a large extent a statement of their relations with each other within the system. Instead of an alphabetical glossary, which would entail much repetition, a diagram has been constructed showing the relative positions in the system of the Transcendental Philosophy of the principal special words and phrases that occur in the *Prolegomena*, together with a few which only occur in the *Critique*. This method of presentation may draw a certain authenticity from Kant's repeated references to the importance of seeing the *Critique* as a whole and of understanding any part of it from its place in the articulation of the whole. This chart (printed overleaf) and the analytical table of contents which follows should make it possible to locate the paragraphs in the *Prolegomena* and should take the place of an index.

THE SYSTEM OF CRITICAL *or* TRANSCENDENTAL IDEALISM (*as in the Prologomena*)

THE TRANSCENDENTAL AESTHETIC	THE TRANSCENDENTAL ANALYTIC	THE TRANSCENDENTAL DIALECTIC
SENSES	UNDERSTANDING	REASON
THE SUBJECT :		
faculty of representation, perception	faculty of judgement	faculty of the unification of the understanding under principles
peculiar way of being affected	way of unifying representations	natural disposition to metaphysics
intuitive, intuits	discursive, judges, thinks through rules and concepts	forms of syllogism
form of sensibility	logical types of judgement, formal conditions of judgements	
pure intuitions of outer senses : space of inner sense : time	the 12 pure concepts, categories, concepts of an object in general, concept of the synthetic unity of intuitions, concepts originally generated in the understanding	ideas of pure reason

PURE or A PRIORI SYNTHESIS (the subject within itself) :

SYNTHETIC JUDGEMENTS A PRIORI :

pure unity of the understanding, principles *or* form of possible experience, universal a priori law of nature

pure intuition m. of extension—geometry arithmetic	(1) mathematical (concerning generation of intuitions by application of mathematics in natural science) : axioms of intuition (quantity) anticipations of perception (quality) (2) dynamic (relations of existences in experience) : analogies of experience (laws of nature) postulates of empirical thought in general (distinction between truth and hypothesis)	perience *or* of complete series of conditions psychological ideas— paralogisms cosmological ideas— antinomy theological idea— ideal of pure reason
THE OBJECT : THINGS IN THEMSELVES (NOUMENA)		
CONTINGENT EMPIRICAL SYNTHESIS (*subject affected by objects*) : THINGS IN THEMSELVES AFFECT THE SENSES, *yielding* representations sensation, empirical intuitions, perceptions appearances, phenomena matter [*as opposed to form*]	(1) REPRESENTATIONS ARE UNIFIED IN A CONSCIOUSNESS, logical connection of perceptions in a thinking subject (without pure concepts), *yielding* : objects, beings of the senses, concepts of objects of intuition judgements of perception—subjectively valid, contingent, a posteriori	—
NECESSARY EMPIRICAL SYNTHESIS (*subject submits its affection by objects to its own pure synthesis*) :	(2) REPRESENTATIONS ARE UNIFIED IN A CONSCIOUSNESS IN GENERAL, intuitions are subsumed under categories by means of schema, *yielding* : outer/inner experience, world, nature judgements of experience—objective, universally valid laws of nature (of outer senses, physics, of inner sense, empirical psychology)	THE (CONSTITUTIVE) USE OF THE UNDERSTANDING IN EXPERIENCE IS REGULATED BY IDEAS OF REASON the world is thought *as if* it were the product of a highest understanding and will

Notes concerning the Translations of certain Terms

At the time when Kant was writing strong objection was felt to the once prevalent use of foreign loan-words in German. Kant translates many Latin and Greek forms into German forms, sometimes also giving the Latin word in parentheses. This normally causes no difficulty, but the following are cases in which comment is required.

' Appearances ' and ' phenomena ' are identical terms. They render *Erscheinungen*, the German form, and *Phaenomena*, the loan-word of which *Erscheinungen* is a translation. The same holds of ' things in themselves ' and ' noumena '.

' Critique ' and ' criticism ' both render *Kritik*. ' Critique of Pure Reason ' was intended by Kant to be the name not merely of a book but of a branch of philosophy, and to have the same kind of usage as ' metaphysics ', ' logic ', etc. There is no textual distinction between the title (' critique ') and the subject, for which ' criticism ' usually seems preferable, and the translator's choice has sometimes been arbitrary.

' Deduce ' and ' deduction ' render both the loan-word *Deduktion*, and its German translation *Ableitung*. Kant usually reserves *Deduktion* for his special sense of the term, akin to ' justification ' (though he once uses the translation), but uses the verbal form *ableiten* both in this special sense and in the usual logical sense of ' deduce ', as well as sometimes using it loosely for ' infer'. We have followed Kant and rendered *ableiten* by ' deduce ' in all cases. The context usually makes the sense clear. Several weaker words that are not technical terms are rendered by ' derive '.

' Enthusiasm ' renders *Schwärmerei*, in spite of the fact that the loan-word written by Kant *Enthusiasm* and *Schwärmerei* are contrasted in a passage in the *Critique of Judgement* (Acad. ed., V. 275) where *Enthusiasm* is said to be comparable with madness and *Schwärmerei* with delirium. *Schwärmerei* is described there as ' the error of trying to *see* something beyond all boundaries of sensibility, i.e. to dream according to principles (to rage rationally) ', which agrees well with its use here. It is rendered by ' enthusiasm ' in contexts such as passages of polemic against enthusiasm, dogmatism, materialism, etc., but other grammatical forms of it are rendered by ' visionary ' (as in ' Berkeley's visionary idealism '), ' extravagant ' and ' fatuous '.

' Principle ' renders both the German word *Grundsatz*, literally ' fundamental proposition ', and the loan-word *Prinzip*. In Kant's own strict usage *Prinzipien* (' principles ') include both fundamental concepts and fundamental propositions (*Grundsätze*), but he does not adhere to this consistently. It should be borne in mind that the word ' principle ' as used here nearly always contains the sense of ' proposition '.

ANALYTICAL TABLE OF CONTENTS

All the headings and sub-headings provided (very erratically) by Kant are retained here, and distinguished by being printed in small capitals. Some further headings, also printed in small capitals but enclosed in square brackets, have been supplied by the translator. The rest is strictly Kant's in matter but the editor's in form.

This table is intended to be used only in conjunction with the text and is not intended to be intelligible independently of it. It may assist the reader to keep the main thread of the argument before him and to assess the relative importance of the parts at the value given to them by Kant. It may also serve in the place of an index.

[PREFACE] (3–14)

[I] Metaphysics, which is in disrepute, is to be suspended and the question asked, whether metaphysics is possible at all ? (3–5) ; the requirements of its possibility having been stated here for the first time, metaphysics must be re-born as a science (5).

[II] Hume's epoch-making discovery : that the *a priori* necessity supposed to lie in the connection of a thing as cause with another as effect cannot be thought ; and his mistake, in inferring that there can be no *a priori* knowledge at all and hence no metaphysics (5–7). He was obstinately misunderstood by the philosophers of common sense (7–9). Kant's advance : to universalise Hume's objection, to discover and deduce a complete list of *a priori* concepts used by the understanding, and thus to determine the extent of pure reason and to establish the possibility of metaphysics (9–10).

[III] Prolixity and dryness, and alleged obscurity (which comes from judging a new science, that had previously been thought impossible, with old ways of thinking), though necessary to the *Critique*, are to be relieved by offering in the *Prolegomena* an analytic plan of what was presented synthetically in the *Critique*. The correctness of the *Critique* will thereby more easily be seen, through surveying more easily the main points and the internal articulation of the parts, there being no means of correcting it from outside (10–14).

PREAMBLE

OF WHAT IS PECULIAR TO ALL METAPHYSICAL KNOWLEDGE (15–26)

§ 1 OF THE SOURCES OF METAPHYSICS : they are *a priori* namely pure understanding and pure reason, not empirical, namely outer and inner experience (15–16).

§ 2 OF THE KIND OF KNOWLEDGE THAT ALONE CAN BE CALLED METAPHYSICAL

a. OF THE DISTINCTION BETWEEN SYNTHETIC AND ANALYTIC JUDGEMENTS IN GENERAL : a distinction according to content between ampliative and explicative judgements (16–17).

b. THE COMMON PRINCIPLE OF ALL ANALYTIC JUDGEMENTS IS THE PRINCIPLE OF CONTRADICTION (17).

c. SYNTHETIC JUDGEMENTS NEED A DIFFERENT PRINCIPLE FROM THE PRINCIPLE OF CONTRADICTION (17–24) : synthetic judgements classified into :

1. judgements of experience (*a posteriori*) (18)

GENERAL QUESTION
IS METAPHYSICS POSSIBLE AT ALL ? (27–29)

GENERAL QUESTION
HOW IS KNOWLEDGE OUT OF PURE REASON POSSIBLE ? (30–35)

(Rational belief, accepting uncriticised metaphysical assumptions for practical guidance, is useful, but as art not science) (33). This solution constitutes transcendental philosophy which must precede all metaphysics (33–34).

The problem will be solved in four stages : how is (i) pure mathematics (ii) pure natural science (iii) metaphysics in general (including metaphysics as a natural disposition), and (iv) metaphysics as science, possible ? (34–35). Answering these questions will incidentally reveal the principles of the correct use of these sciences (35).

MAIN TRANSCENDENTAL QUESTION, FIRST PART

HOW IS PURE MATHEMATICS POSSIBLE ? (36–51)

§ 6 Examination of mathematics, which is apodictic, pure and synthetic, might reveal an *a priori* ground of knowledge (36).

§ 7 Mathematics must exhibit its concept in intuition (' construct ' it)—(philosophy, by contrast, is not intuitive but discursive)—hence, being pure and *a priori*, in pure intuition (36–37). § 8 Intuition *a priori*, i.e. without the presence of an object, at first sight impossible (37–38) § 9 (and wholly impossible if intuition represented to us things in themselves), is possible only if it contains nothing but the form of sensibility in us as subject (and hence is only valid for objects of our senses) (38) ; § 10 synthetic propositions *a priori* are possible only if this is presupposed (38–39). The pure intuitions are space (for geometry) and time (for arithmetic) (39). § 11 The solution to the problem ' how is pure mathematics possible ? ' is that pure mathematics (i) only bears on the form of appearances, (ii) the empirical intuition of which is grounded in a pure intuition which is the form of our sensibility (39–40).

§ 12 Examples from geometry : proofs of congruence of figures and of three-dimensionality rest on intuition and are not deducible from concepts ; nor is projection to infinity of line or motion, which presupposes space and time as unbounded, i.e. as in intuition (40–41). § 13 Spherical triangles, mirror images, left and right hand gloves, symmetrical helices, can be identical as to thinkable determinations, yet not interchangeable ; they are distinguishable only by means of their relation to space as a whole, i.e. to intuition, which could not be the case with things in themselves (41–43).

NOTE I Geometry has objective reality as prescribing the form of all sensible intuition ; if the senses represented to us things in themselves, geometry would be fiction (43–45).

NOTE II Idealism asserts that only thinking beings exist. Kant asserts on the contrary that bodies exist outside us and affect our sensibility, but that all their known properties (not merely secondary, as for Locke, but also primary) belong merely to our representations (45–46).

NOTE III The objection that the ideality of space and time turns the world of the senses into illusion is vain. Not appearance to the senses, but judgement by the understanding (i.e. combination of representations in the concept of an object) is true or false. Whether space is appearance or thing in itself has no bearing on this (46–48) ; but the doctrine that space is appearance secures the objective validity of geometry and prevents the transcendent illusion of the antinomy of reason (48–50). To avoid further confusion with the idealism of Descartes and Berkeley, Kant prefers to call his system critical (instead of transcendental) idealism (50–51).

MAIN TRANSCENDENTAL QUESTION, SECOND PART
HOW IS PURE NATURAL SCIENCE POSSIBLE ? (52–89)

§ 14 (i) Nature (considered formally) is existence determined according to universal laws (not existence of things in themselves, for that could be known neither *a priori*, because if the understanding had to conform to things in themselves it could not do so *before* they were given, nor *a posteriori*, because if the laws taught by experience had to apply to things in themselves they would have to be necessary laws, but they are not) (52). § 15 There are in fact such universal *a priori* laws of nature. 'General natural science' contains mathematics applied to appearances and some philosophical (discursive) principles; though it includes some not wholly pure concepts (e.g. motion, impenetrability, inertia, etc.) and confines itself to objects of the outer senses, it contains some genuinely universal *a priori* principles (e.g. substance is permanent, every event is previously determined by a cause according to constant laws) (53).

§ 16 (ii) Nature (considered materially) is the totality of all objects of experience (not of objects outside experience, for we are only concerned with confirmable *a priori* knowledge) (53–54).

§ 17 The question can be framed as : how is it possible for *either* (i) things as objects of experience *or* (ii) experience of objects to be known *a priori* to have necessary conformity to law ? These are equivalent because the subjective laws of experience are also valid of objects as experienced. The second is more convenient (54–56).

§ 18 Empirical judgements merely subjectively valid are judgements of perception ; objectively valid (for everyone always), they are judgements of experience, and require pure concepts of the understanding. Objective validity means agreement with the object, which means necessary universality ; § 19 the first and last are identical concepts (56–57). Objective validity of judgement (connection of perceptions) rests on conditions of the objective validity of the connection, not on empirical or sensible conditions, i.e. on a pure concept of the understanding. Subjective judgements : things are warm, sweet, nasty, air is elastic (57–58). § 20 To turn judgements of perception into judgements of experience, perceptions must be joined not merely in consciousness, but in a consciousness in general, i.e. subsumed under a pure concept of the understanding, e.g. cause (air is elastic necessarily ; the sun shines, the stone grows warm—the sun warms the stone) (58-60). All objective synthetic judgements include such a concept, even the axioms of pure mathematics (60-61).

§ 21 Logical table of judgements, transcendental table of pure concepts of the understanding (categories), and pure physiological table of the universal principles of natural science (61-62).

§ 21a Résumé : experience consists of intuition (from sensibility) plus judgement (from the understanding), the judgement being determined as necessary by the addition of a concept of the synthetic unity of intuitions (63).

§ 22 Second résumé : the senses intuit, the understanding thinks, i.e. unifies representations in a consciousness, either subjectively and contingently or objectively and necessarily ; the logical moments of all judgements are the possible ways of unifying representations in a consciousness, and if used as concepts, are concepts of the necessary [1] unification of representations. The unification is either analytic (of identical representations) or synthetic (of different representations) ; experience consists in synthetic necessary connection of appearances in a consciousness, and is generated by subsuming them under pure concepts of the understanding (63). § 23 There are no conditions of experience above those of subsumption under pure concepts, therefore these are the *a priori* principles of possible experience and universal laws of nature (65).

The question ' how is pure natural science possible ? ' is thus solved : the formal conditions of all judgements constitute a logical system ; the concepts grounded therein (*a priori* conditions of necessary judgements) constitute a transcendental system ; the principles for subsuming appearances under these concepts constitute a physiological system (system of nature), and this is pure natural science (65-66).

[1] Because these are the *only* possible ways.—*Ed.*

§§ 24–26

§ 24 The reader is referred by Kant to the Analytic of
Principles in the *Critique* (66).

The first two principles (axioms of intuition and anticipations of perception) are principles of the application of
mathematics to experience (66–67). § 25 The third and
fourth principles (analogies of experience and postulates of
empirical thought in general) are *dynamic*, being principles
of the relation of appearances in experience—either their
relation among themselves, when they must be subsumed
under the analogies (the concepts of thing (substance), of
succession (cause), or of contemporaneity (community)) ;
or their relation to experience in general (the postulates
—possibility, reality, necessity) (67–68).

§ 26 The principles being drawn from the understanding
itself, (i) the table is known to be a complete table of all
synthetic principles *a priori*, (ii) they apply only in possible
experience, not to things in themselves, (iii) they are proved
by reference to the form of possible experience and to existence in time in general (pure unity of the understanding),
i.e. neither to the matter of experience (appearances) nor
to things in themselves (68–70).

§§ 27–31

§ 27 Hume asserted that causality (the existence of a
thing necessarily posited by the existence of another thing)
is unintelligible ; Kant adds that substance (necessary
ground of existence) and community (necessary interde-
pendence of substances) are also unintelligible. But they
are not illusory, as for Hume, but proved objectively correct
by Kant (though only in respect of possible experience),
§ 28 by showing that they are concepts of connections, not
between things in themselves, but between representations

in a judgement, and that without them we could have no knowledge of objects (70–72). § 29 Hume's crux : Cause. The hypothetical judgement expressing subjective connection of perceptions (if the sun shines on it, the body grows warm) is turned into universal law (thus making experience possible) by adding necessity (sun is the cause of heat). Cause is a form of possible experience, not an aspect of the thing in itself (72–73). § 30 The pure concepts of the understanding have no objective reality outside experience. They are not, as for Hume, drawn from experience but experience is drawn from them. All synthetic principles *a priori* are nothing more than principles of possible experience (73–74). § 31 Polemic against dogmatic metaphysics, common sense, probability, reasonable conjecture and analogy (74–75).

§§ 32–35 [NOUMENA] (75–79)

§ 32 To admit appearances is to admit the existence of noumena (beings of the understanding) which affect our senses, but we can-know nothing determinate about them (75–76). § 33 The fact that the pure concepts are not drawn from experience is a temptation to use them transcendently (76–77). § 34 Reference to the *Critique* on (i) the schematism and (ii) the ground of the distinction between phenomena and noumena. ((i) The senses only provide schemata for the pure concepts, not these concepts *in concreto*, and (ii) an intelligible world is a problem soluble only to an intuitive understanding) (77–78). § 35 The extravagance of the understanding, in going beyond experience, can only be cured by scientifically proving dogmatic metaphysics impossible (78–79).

§§ 36–38 HOW IS NATURE ITSELF POSSIBLE ? (79–84)

§ 36 (i) materially, as the totality of appearances : through the peculiar quality of our senses, to be affected by unknown objects (Transcendental Aesthetic and First Main Question).

(ii) formally, as the totality of rules for possible experience : through the peculiar quality of our understanding, to think through rules (Transcendental Logic and Second Main Question).

These qualities cannot be further analysed because experience and thought are impossible without them.

The possibility of experience in general (the conditions of necessary unification in a consciousness) is the same as the universal *a priori* laws of nature, which are not drawn from nature but prescribed to nature by the understanding (79–82).

§ 37 Examples : § 38 circle, cone and sphere : the laws of their properties in geometry and astronomy are deducible from the concepts (of equal radii etc.) according to which the understanding constructed them, and are not taken from the figure or from space independently of the understanding.

The unity of objects is determined solely by the understanding ; the world of the senses is either not an object of experience at all, or is nature (82–84).

§ 39 APPENDIX TO PURE NATURAL SCIENCE
OF THE SYSTEM OF THE CATEGORIES

The pure concepts of the understanding (categories) make a system known to be complete since deduced from one principle (unlike Aristotle's categories) (84–85). The principle was found by (i) eliminating space and time (ii) finding a comprehensive act of the understanding which contains all others, viz. judging (iii) taking in logic and making a complete table of functions of judging (iv) referring these to the conditions of objective validity of judgements, thereby producing the pure concepts (system of transcendental philosophy) (85–86). (After completing the system, Predicables, made by combining categories with each other and with space and time, are to be added) (86, 88 n.).

The essential thing about the categories is that they are

logical functions, not concepts of objects ; through hitherto lacking this insight, metaphysics has been pernicious (86-87). The system of categories, being exhaustive, makes any consequent metaphysical enquiry systematic and ejects alien concepts (e.g. ideas of reason, previously confused with concepts of the understanding) (87-89).

Main Transcendental Question, third part
How is metaphysics possible in general ?
(90–133)

§ 40 Metaphysics has to do essentially with ideas derived out of reason itself and not given in or confirmable by experience, but needed for the problem of the absolute whole of all possible experience, which is not itself experience. These ideas may mislead in that they are mistakenly supposed to refer to objects whereas this deduction shows that they only concern the guidance of reason itself in its immanent use (90–91). § 41 This distinction between categories and ideas is the foundation of metaphysics as science (92). § 42 The use of ideas can only be corrected from within reason itself (92).

§ 43 The functions of the syllogism, being the only possible forms of all judgements of the understanding, would be the origin whence the ideas of reason might be known completely (93–94) :—

functions of syllogism	idea		giving rise to the dialectic of
categorical	of the complete subject	psychological	the paralogism of p. r.
hypothetical	of the complete series of conditions	cosmological	the antinomy of p. r.
disjunctive	of a complete totality of the possible	theological	the ideal of p. r.

§ 44 The ideas are of no use to the understanding for experience (e.g. the soul a simple substance, the beginning of the world, explanation of nature from the will of a highest being), but reason contributes to the perfection of the understanding in that it demands completeness in the use of the understanding in experience. Reason has to think this completeness as if it were an object, whereas it is only an idea (94–95).

The Dialectic of Pure Reason

§ 45 Preliminary Remark : The understanding may be enticed by reason to a transcendent use, which must be prevented by scientific instruction (96–97).

§§ 46–49 I. Psychological Ideas (Paralogisms) : § 46 The understanding being discursive, i.e. thinking through concepts (predicates), substance, i.e. the absolute subject devoid of predicates, is unthinkable by us. In the case of consciousness of self, the absolute subject (ego) seems to be given in intuition ; but the ego is not a concept, and only designates the reference of inner appearances to their unknown subject (97–98). § 47 Its permanence cannot be proved from the idea itself of the soul as substance, but only in possible experience, § 48 i.e. in life (98–100). § 49 The existence of outside objects as appearances in space is proved from outer experience in the same way as that of the soul as an inner state in time from inner experience (100–101). Cartesian idealism is overcome by this transcendental or formal idealism (101–102).

§§ 50–54 II. Cosmological Ideas (Antinomies) § 50 extend the connection of conditions beyond experience (102–103). § 51 They contain four antinomies corresponding to the four classes of categories : (i) the world is limited/infinite in time and space (ii) the world consists of simples/composites (iii) there is freedom/only nature in the world (iv) there is a necessary being as cause of the world/there is none (103–104). § 52 If the principles of appearances are taken as valid of things in themselves, both members of each can be proved (103–105).

§ 52b This reveals an incorrectness (otherwise hidden) in the presuppositions of reason (105–106). § 52c In the first two (mathematical) antinomies both thesis and anti-thesis are false, and have as their ground the contradictory concept of a thing in itself in space and time (106–108). § 53 In the third and fourth (dynamic) antinomies, both thesis and antithesis may be true, and are mistakenly held to be contradictory. Heterogeneity between cause (thing in itself) and effect (appearance) is permissible. Natural necessity refers to appearances, freedom to things in themselves. Freedom, to be a property of causes, must be spontaneous causation and thus noumenal, since appearance only has chains of causation in time ; the same thing can be both free (as thing in itself) and naturally caused (as appearance) without contradiction. Freedom holds of the *relation* of the intellectual as cause to appearance as effect, i.e. neither of matter alone nor of God alone (108–110). The connection of man with objective (noumenal) grounds is expressed by *ought*, the faculty of this is reason, and the causality of reason, freedom. Causation through freedom, which is not in time, cannot hinder natural necessity, which is in time (110–112). The fourth antinomy is solved in the same way : causes are conditioned as appearances, but there is an absolute cause as thing in itself (112–113). § 54 Assent to these solutions will come with growing familiarity with the concepts of the *Critique* (113).

§ 55 III. THEOLOGICAL IDEA (Ideal of Pure Reason) : The necessary hypothesis of a perfect original being taken as a dogma. Kant has nothing to add to what he has said in the Critique about transcendental theology (114).

§ 56 GENERAL NOTE TO THE TRANSCENDENTAL IDEAS : In nature much is inconceivable, but in pure reason nothing can be, since its ideas come from within itself. The problems of reason are solved by showing that its ideas are principles for establishing unanimity, completeness and synthetic unity in the use of the understanding, i.e. are regulative, not constitutive (114–116).

§§ 57–59 CONCLUSION

OF THE DETERMINATION OF THE BOUNDARIES OF
PURE REASON (116–130)

§ 57 To admit no noumena or to declare our experience,
spatial and temporal intuition, and discursive understanding the only possible kind of knowledge and experience, is
to make the principles of our experience transcendent, and
the limits of our reason the limits of things in themselves
(as in Hume's *Dialogues concerning Natural Religion*). To
avoid scepticism as well as confusion in science, the
boundaries of the use of reason must be formally determined (116–118).

Experience, as raising an uncompletable series of questions (concerning the soul, the world and God), can never
satisfy reason (118–119). Boundaries presuppose an en-
closing space, limits are merely negative and do not. In
mathematics and natural science reason knows limits
(restriction to appearances) but no boundaries (new knowledge extends to infinity) ; in metaphysics reason has not
merely limits but boundaries indicated by the transcendental ideas (ideas of completion of the series of conditions)
(119–121). Here is a real connection between the known
and the unknown (noumenon), the idea of which is needed
by reason but must only be thought by concepts of its
relation to the world of the senses (121–122). Example :
the highest being. Understanding and will are not
attributable to it, since my concepts of these are dependent
on human experience. Hume's sound objections to such
anthropomorphism in theism. But the transcendent and
immanent can subsist together *on* the boundary of reason
by means of concepts of the relation of the highest being
to the world. We can allow ourselves *symbolic* (but not
dogmatic) anthropomorphism : to regard the world *as if*
it were the product of understanding and will, i.e. the
world is related to the unknown as clock etc. to the artisan
etc. (122–124).

§ 58 Vindication of theism against Hume. This is knowledge by analogy (similarity of relations between dissimilars). Granted an original being (deistic concept), causality through reason (theism) can be predicated of its relation to the world analogically, as cause of the rationality of the world (to permit fullest use of reason in the world), but reason must not be predicated of the being itself as efficient cause acting by means of the will (to avoid hyperphysical explanation of appearances). We think of the world *as if* it stemmed from a highest reason. To the (antidogmatic) principle of not forcing reason outside experience must be joined the (anti-sceptical) principle of not regarding experience as setting its own boundaries (125–128).

§ 59 Knowledge of the boundary is genuine knowledge. Natural theology is such. The proposition that reason can only teach us what is known in possible experience is not infringed by the reference on the boundary to something beyond experience, teaching us how to regulate the use of reason, which is all we could wish for (128–130).

§ 60

[THE NATURAL ENDS OF THE DISPOSITION TO METAPHYSICS]

This question belongs not to metaphysics but to anthropology. The end is that reason, by seeing a field of objects of pure understanding, should reach the universality it needs for its practical (moral) principles. The psychological idea prevents materialism, the cosmological idea, naturalism, and the theological idea, fatalism. Two scholia : (1) the question of the use of metaphysics, belonging to philosophy (the unity of the speculative and practical uses of reason) (ii) the question proposed but not solved in the Critique, of the regulative use of reason in natural science (130–133).

SOLUTION TO THE GENERAL QUESTION OF THE
PROLEGOMENA

HOW IS METAPHYSICS POSSIBLE AS A SCIENCE ? (134–141)

A critique of reason which exhibits (i) all the *a priori*
concepts, classified and analysed, (ii) a deduction of them
which shows the possibility of synthetic knowledge *a priori*,
and (iii) the principles and boundaries of their use, all this
in a complete system, makes metaphysics possible as a
science. This having now been done, the only question
is how to get the job started (134).

Nausea at dogmatic metaphysics will be replaced by
delight in the permanent completeness of scientific metaphysics, which is possible because reason here draws its
knowledge not from objects but from within itself (134–135).
The time for the destruction of dogmatic metaphysics
has arrived, as is shown by present indifference to it ; the
re-birth of metaphysics is still to come, necessarily, as
metaphysics is a necessity of life (136–137). Existing
metaphysics contains useful preparatory analyses of concepts, but nothing synthetic. Polemic against the grounding of synthetic propositions *a priori* on probability and on
common sense (which can only understand instances, not
rules). The propositions of mathematics supposedly self-
evident to common sense are irrelevant to metaphysics,
since ' constructed '. Probability and common sense are
legitimate and wholesome in rational belief (137–141).

APPENDIX

OF WHAT CAN BE DONE TO MAKE METAPHYSICS
AS A SCIENCE REAL

This essay, offering to do this, deserves to be examined
with care. It can be judged either from outside (but this
is illegitimate, since metaphysics has no certain established
criteria) or from inside. Examples of each follow
(142–143).

[i] SPECIMEN OF A JUDGEMENT ON THE CRITIQUE WHICH

PRECEDES ENQUIRY. Polemic against the [Garve-Feder] review (143-145). Genuine idealism from the Eleatics to Berkeley asserts that knowledge from experience is illusion, and from pure reason, truth ; Kant's idealism asserts that knowledge from pure reason is illusion, and from experience, truth. Berkeley, failing to recognise space as known *a priori* (and ignoring time), had no criteria (universal laws) of the truth of experience, which was therefore illusion. Idealism has always postulated intellectual intuition through failing to see that the senses can intuit *a priori*. Kant's idealism, which secures the objective reality of *a priori* knowledge, to be called formal or critical idealism, to distinguish it from that of Berkeley and Descartes (145-146). Further polemic (146-151).

[ii] PROPOSAL FOR AN EXAMINATION OF THE CRITIQUE ON WHICH A JUDGEMENT CAN FOLLOW. Allusion to a favorable [Gotha] review (151). Kant proposes a co-operative investigation of the *Critique*, using the *Prolegomena* as guide, in order to have Kant's or other critical principles established (152-154). The metaphysics that would follow would render real service to the public and would render theology safe from enthusiasm disguised as dogmatic speculation (154-155).

INDEX OF NAMES

*On the opposite page is printed a translation
of the title page of the original editions*

PROLEGOMENA

to

any

FUTURE METAPHYSICS

that

will be able to present itself

AS A SCIENCE

by

IMMANUEL KANT

Riga

Johann Friedrich Hartknoch

1783

NOTE

Kant's footnotes are shown by asterisks, the translator's by numerals. The pagination of the Berlin Academy edition of the Collected Works, Vol. IV, is shown in square brackets on left-hand pages.

[PREFACE [1]]

[I]

These Prolegomena are not for the use of pupils but of future teachers, and they are intended to be of service to them not for arranging their exposition of an existing science, but for making their first discovery of this science itself.

There are scholars for whom the history of philosophy (ancient as well as modern) is itself their philosophy ; for these the present prolegomena are not written. They must wait until those who are at pains to draw from the springs of reason itself have made out their case ; then it will be their turn to give the world news of what has happened. Otherwise nothing can be said which in their opinion has not been said before ; and this may in fact hold for everything future, as an infallible prediction. For as the human understanding has been roving over countless objects in many different ways for many centuries, it cannot easily fail to happen that for everything new something old should be found, that has some similarity with it.

My purpose is to convince all those who find it worth their while to occupy themselves with metaphysics : that it is absolutely necessary to suspend their work for the present, to regard everything that has happened hitherto as not having happened, and before all else first to raise the question : ' whether such a thing as metaphysics is possible at all.'

If it is a science, how does it come about that it cannot establish itself, like other sciences, in universal and lasting esteem ? If it is not, how does it happen that under the semblance of a science it ceaselessly gives itself airs and

[1] In the original editions there is no heading. This opening section corresponds in manner to the Prefaces of the Critiques. The subdivision into three parts, numbered I–III, has also been supplied by the translator.

keeps the human understanding in suspense with hopes that never fade and are never fulfilled ? Whether we demonstrate our knowledge or our ignorance, something certain must at last be settled about the nature of this would-be science ; for things cannot possibly go on any longer on their present footing. It seems almost ridiculous, while every other science makes ceaseless progress, to be constantly turning round on the same spot without moving a step forward in the one that claims to be wisdom itself and whose oracle everyone consults. Also it has lost a great many of its supporters, and we do not see those who feel themselves strong enough to shine in other sciences wanting to risk their reputation in this one, in which everyone who is ignorant in all other things arrogates to himself a decisive judgement ; for there is in fact no sure weight and measure as yet in this territory with which to distinguish soundness from shallow chatter.

But when a science has been worked on for a long time and people are full of wonder at the progress it has made, it is not anything so unheard of that someone should finally let it occur to him to ask : whether and how in general such a science is possible. For human reason is so eager to build that several times already it has finished the tower and has dismantled it again afterwards, to see what its foundations might be like. It is never too late to grow rational and wise ; but it is always harder, if the insight comes late, to get it under way.

To ask : whether a science is possible, presupposes that the reality of the science is in doubt. But such a doubt offends everyone whose entire goods and chattels may perhaps consist in this supposed jewel ; and hence the man who permits himself to utter this doubt should be prepared for resistance from all sides. Some, proudly conscious of their old and hence supposedly legitimate possession, with their metaphysical compendia in their hand, will look down on him and despise him ; others, who nowhere see anything that is not the same as something they have already seen

4

somewhere else, will not understand him ; and everything will go on for a time as if nothing had occurred that might give occasion for fear or hope of an imminent change.

None the less I venture to predict that the reader of these prolegomena who thinks for himself will not only have doubts as to his previous science, but in the sequel will be wholly convinced that there cannot be such a science unless the demands expressed here, on which its possibility rests, are fulfilled ; and as this has never yet happened, that there is as yet no metaphysics at all. But as enquiry for it can never die away *, because the interest of universal human reason is much too intimately interwoven with it, the reader will admit that a complete reform or rather a re-birth of metaphysics, according to a hitherto quite unknown plan, is inevitably imminent, however much it may for a time be resisted.

[II]

Since LOCKE's and LEIBNIZ's Essays,[1] or rather since the beginning of metaphysics as far as the history of it reaches, no event has occurred which could have been more decisive in respect of the fate of this science than the attack which DAVID HUME made on it. He brought no light into this kind of knowledge, but he struck a spark at which a light could well have been kindled, if it had found a receptive tinder and if the glow had been carefully kept up and increased.

HUME started in the main from a single but important concept in metaphysics, namely that of the *connection of cause and effect* (together with its consequential concepts of

* Rusticus exspectat, dum defluat amnis : at ille
  Labitur et labetur in omne volubilis aevum.

                                                    Horat.[2]

---

[1] i.e. Locke's *Essay concerning Human Understanding* (1690), translated into French, Latin and German by 1757 ; and Leibniz's *Nouveaux Essais sur l'entendement humain,* first published posthumously in 1765.

[2] Horace : *Epist.* I. 2. 42 f. " The peasant waits for the river to flow away, but it glides along and will roll along to all eternity."

force and action etc.). He challenged Reason, who pretends to have conceived this concept in her womb, to give an account of herself and say with what right she thinks : that anything can be of such a nature, that if it is posited, something else must thereby also be posited necessarily ; for that is what the concept of cause says. He proved irrefutably : that it is wholly impossible for reason to think such a conjunction *a priori* and out of concepts. For this conjunction contains necessity ; but it is quite impossible to see how, because something is, something else must also necessarily be, and how therefore the concept of such an *a priori* connection can be introduced. From this he inferred that Reason completely deceives herself with this concept, in falsely taking it for her own child, whereas it is nothing but a bastard of the imagination fathered by experience. The imagination, having by experience brought certain representations under the law of association, passes off a subjective necessity arising out of this, namely custom, for an objective necessity from insight. From this he inferred : reason has no power to think such connections, not even only to think them universally, because its concepts would then be mere fictions, and all its ostensibly *a priori* knowledge is nothing but falsely stamped ordinary experiences ; which is as much as to say that there is no metaphysics at all, and cannot be any.*

---

* None the less HUME called this destructive philosophy itself metaphysics, and attached a high value to it. " Metaphysics and morals, he says (Essays, 4th part, p. 214, German translation),[1] are the most important branches of science ; mathematics and natural science are not worth half so much." But the sagacious man was here only looking to the negative utility that the moderation of the exaggerated claims of speculative reason would have, in completely putting an end to so many endless and troublesome disputes that confuse the human species ; but he lost sight of the positive damage that arises from depriving reason of its most important prospects, by which alone it can mark out for the will the highest aim of all its endeavours.

---

[1] Hume : *Essays Moral Political and Literary*, edited by T. H. Green.

Hasty and incorrect as was his conclusion, it was at least founded on enquiry, and this enquiry surely made it worth while for the best brains of his time to have come together to solve the problem in the sense in which he expounded it, if possible more happily, and out of this a complete reform of the science must soon have arisen.

But fate, ever unkind to metaphysics, decreed that he should be understood by nobody. One cannot observe without feeling a certain pain, how his opponents REID, OSWALD, BEATTIE [1] and finally PRIESTLEY, [2] so entirely missed the point of his problem. By always taking for granted what he was doubting and on the other hand proving, with violence and often with great unseemliness, what it had never entered his mind to doubt, they so mistook his hint as to how to improve matters that everything remained as it was, as if nothing had happened. The question was not whether the concept of cause is correct, useful, and in respect of all knowledge of nature indispensable, for this HUME had never held in doubt; but whether it is thought

and T. H. Grose, London, 1875, Vol. I, p. 187. Essay XIV: Of the Rise and Progress of the Arts and Sciences.

"Not to mention, that monarchies, receiving their chief stability from a superstitious reverence to priests and princes, have commonly abridged the liberty of reasoning, with regard to religion, and politics, and consequently metaphysics and morals. All these form the most considerable branches of science. Mathematics and natural philosophy, which only remain, are not half so valuable."

[1] Scottish philosophers of common sense and opponents of Hume. Works with German translations available when the *Prolegomena* were being written :—

Thomas Reid : *An Inquiry into the Human Mind on the Principles of Common Sense* (1764), German, 1782.

James Oswald : *An Appeal to Common Sense in behalf of Religion* (1766), German, 1774.

James Beattie : *An Essay on the Nature and Immutability of Truth in opposition to Sophistry and Scepticism* (1770), German, 1772.

[2] Joseph Priestley (the celebrated scientist) : *Letters to a philosophical Unbeliever* (1780), German, 1782. There was no contemporary German translation of his *Examination of Dr. Reid's Inquiry . . ., Dr. Beattie's Essay . . ., and Dr. Oswald's Appeal . . .*, published in 1774.

a priori by reason, and in this way has an inner truth independent of all experience, and hence also has a more widely extended usefulness, not limited merely to objects of experience ; this was the question on which HUME expected enlightenment. He was only talking about the origin of this concept, not about its indispensability in use ; once the former were determined, the conditions of its use and the extent of its validity would have been settled automatically.

But the opponents of the illustrious man would have had to penetrate very deeply into the nature of reason in so far as it is occupied merely with pure thought in order to do justice to this problem ; and this was not to their liking. They therefore discovered a more convenient way to be obstinate and defiant without any insight, namely by appealing to *common sense*. It is in fact a great gift of heaven, to possess right (or as it has recently been called, simple) common sense. But one must prove it by deeds, by the considered and rational things one thinks and says, not by appealing to it like an oracle when one cannot produce anything sensible with which to justify oneself. When insight and science are on the decline, then and no sooner to appeal to common sense is one of the subtle inventions of recent times, by which the stalest windbag can confidently take up with the soundest thinker and hold his own with him. As long as the least remnant of insight remains, we shall do well to take no recourse to this desperate aid. And seen in the light of day this is nothing but an appeal to the judgement of the crowd—applause at which the philosopher blushes but the popular coxcomb struts and triumphs. I should have thought that HUME had as good a claim to sound sense as BEATTIE, and on top of this to something that BEATTIE certainly did not possess, namely a critical reason, which keeps common sense within limits, so that it does not soar into speculation and lose itself, or if speculations alone are at issue, does not try to decide anything, not knowing how to justify itself concerning its own principles ; for only thus will it remain sound sense.[1] Hammer and chisel will serve very well for a piece of carpentry, but for copper-plate one must use an etching-needle. Common sense and speculation are both useful, but each in its own way ; the one, when we are concerned with judgements that are to find immediate application in experience, the other when judgements are to be made universally, out of mere concepts, for example in metaphysics, in which sound sense, self-styled but often *per antiphrasin*, has no judgement whatever.

I freely admit : it was DAVID HUME's remark that first, many years ago, interrupted my dogmatic slumber and gave a completely different direction to my enquiries in the field of speculative philosophy. I was very far from listening to him in respect of his conclusions, which were merely the result of his not representing his problem to himself as a whole, and instead only lighting on part of it, which can give no information without taking the whole into account. When we begin from a thought well-grounded but not worked out which another has bequeathed to us, we may well hope through continued reflection to advance beyond the point reached by the sagacious man whom we have to thank for the first spark of this light.

So I tried first whether HUME's objection could not be represented universally, and I soon found that the concept of the connection of cause and effect is by no means the only one by which connections between things are thought *a priori* by the understanding ; indeed that metaphysics consists of nothing else whatever. I tried to make certain of the number of these concepts, and when I had succeeded in doing this in the way I wished, namely from a single principle, I proceeded to the deduction of them. I was

---

[1] lit. " sound understanding ". The word translated in this paragraph as " sense " is the word (*Verstand*) which is elsewhere translated " understanding ". In using this word Kant is able to allude simultaneously to the philosophy of common sense and to his own doctrine of the limitation of the understanding to experience.

now assured that they are not, as HUME had feared, deduced from experience, but have their origin in pure understanding. This deduction, which seemed impossible to my sagacious predecessor, and had never even occurred to anyone except him, although everyone confidently used these concepts without asking on what their objective validity is grounded—this deduction, I say, was the most difficult thing that could ever be undertaken on behalf of metaphysics ; and, worst of all, any metaphysics that there is anywhere at all could not give me the slightest help, because this deduction has first to establish the possibility of a metaphysics. Having succeeded in solving HUME's problem not merely in a special case, but with regard to the whole faculty of pure reason, I could take sure although still only slow steps towards determining at last the whole extent of pure reason, completely and according to universal principles, in its boundaries as well as in its content. This is what metaphysics needs in order to construct its system according to a sure plan.

[III]

But I fear that the *working out* of HUME's problem in its greatest possible extension (namely in the Critique of pure Reason) may fare the same as the *problem* itself fared when it was first presented. It will be wrongly judged through not being understood ; and it will not be understood because people will be willing to skim through the pages of the book but not to think through it, and they will not want to spend this trouble on it because the work is dry, because it is obscure, because it is contrary to all ordinary ideas, and on top of that prolix. Now I admit that I do not expect to hear complaints from a philosopher about not being popular, entertaining and agreeable, when it is a matter of the very existence of a highly prized mode of knowledge, indispensable to humanity, which cannot be settled except according to the strictest rules of scholarly exactitude. This may eventually be followed by popularity, but can never begin with it. Yet as regards a certain obscurity deriving in part from the prolixity of the plan, which makes it difficult to survey the main points which are important for the enquiry : on this score the complaint is just, and I shall meet it with the present *Prolegomena*.

The former work, which exhibits the pure faculty of reason in its whole extent and boundaries, always remains the foundation to which the prolegomena refer as mere preliminary exercises ; for that critique must exist as a science, systematic and complete to its smallest parts, before one can think of allowing metaphysics to make its appearance, or even have a remote hope of so doing.

We have long been used to seeing old worn-out modes of knowledge newly trimmed by being taken out of their former contexts and fitted out with a systematic dress according to a personal choice of cut, but with new titles ; and the majority of readers will not anticipate anything else from the critique. But these prolegomena will give them the insight that it is a wholly new science which no-one had previously even thought of, even the mere idea of which was unknown, and towards which nothing of all that has hitherto been done could be used, except the hint that HUME's doubt could give. He likewise suspected nothing of such a possible formal science but put his ship aground, to bring it into safety, on the shore of scepticism where it may lie and rot ; instead of which what I want to do is to give it a pilot who will be able to sail the ship safely wherever he will, using sure principles of navigation drawn from knowledge of the globe, and equipped with a complete set of charts and a compass.

A new science, which is wholly isolated and the only one of its kind, may be approached with the prejudice that it can be judged by means of the supposed knowledge that one already possesses, even though it is the reality of this very knowledge which must first be wholly doubted. To do this only produces the belief that what is seen on all sides is what was already known before, perhaps because the terms sound rather similar.   Yet everything must seem extremely distorted, nonsensical and like gibberish, because it is not the thoughts of the author that are being taken as the basis, but only one's own way of thinking which by long habit has become second nature.   But the prolixity of the work, in so far as it is grounded in the science itself and not in the exposition, its unavoidable dryness and scholastic exactitude, are properties that may greatly benefit the cause, even. though they are bound to be damaging to the book itself.

It is not given to everyone to write as subtly and yet at the same time as attractively as DAVID HUME, or as soundly and yet as elegantly as MOSES MENDELSSOHN[1]; but I could have given my discourse popularity (as I flatter myself) if I had only wanted to devise a plan and to recommend its execution to others, and if I had not had at heart the well-being of the science that kept me occupied for so long ; incidentally, it needed much constancy and even not a little self-denial to put the prospect of late but lasting praise before the attraction of an earlier favorable reception.

Making plans is often a luxuriant, boastful occupation of the mind by which a man gives himself the airs of creative genius, demanding what he cannot perform himself, censuring what he cannot do better, and proposing what he himself does not know where to look for ; though even a mere plan, to be fit for a universal critique of reason, would have needed more than one might guess if it was to be more than the usual recital of pious wishes.   But the sphere of pure reason is so isolated and so thoroughly interconnected within itself that one cannot touch any part of it without touching all the rest, and cannot accomplish anything

[1] Moses Mendelssohn (1729-1786) the most distinguished and successful popular philosophical writer of the German Enlightenment, with a copious literary production from 1755 onwards. His *Treatise on Evidence in the metaphysical Sciences* received the Berlin Academy prize in 1764 for which Kant also competed.

without having previously determined the place of each part and its influence on the others. As there is nothing outside pure reason which could correct our judgement within it, the validity and use of every part depends on its relation within reason itself to the other parts, and, as in the structure of an organised body, the purpose of every member can only be deduced from the complete concept of the whole. Hence it can be said of such a critique that it is never reliable unless it is *whole* and *completed* down to the smallest elements of pure reason, and that in the sphere of this faculty one must determine and settle either *everything* or *nothing*.

But even though a mere plan, if it preceded the Critique of pure Reason, would be unintelligible, unreliable and useless, it is on the other hand so much the more useful when it comes after. For it puts one in a position to survey the whole, to test one by one the main points that are important in this science, and to arrange some things better as regards the exposition than could happen in the first version of the work.

Here then is such a *plan*, coming after the completed work. As I was compelled to compose the work itself according to the *synthetic method*, the plan may now be arranged according to the *analytic method*, so that the science shall display all its articulations, as the structure of a quite peculiar faculty of knowledge, in their natural combination. Whoever finds this plan obscure in its turn, which as prolegomena I am putting at the head of all future metaphysics, should consider that there is no need for everybody to study metaphysics, and that there are many talents which manage very well in sound and even profound sciences that are nearer to intuition, but which do not succeed in researches with nothing but abstract concepts ; and in such a case one should apply one's mental gifts to another object. But whoever finds this plan obscure should also consider that anyone who undertakes to judge a metaphysics, or even to write one, is bound to satisfy the demands that are made here, either by accepting my solution or by soundly refuting it and putting another in its place—for he cannot turn them aside ; and that in the end the obscurity which is so much decried (an accustomed cloak for one's own laziness or stupidity) also has its utility : for all who observe a cautious silence in respect of the other sciences speak with the voice of a master in questions of metaphysics which they brazenly decide, because their ignorance does not of course stand out clearly in metaphysics against the knowledge of others ; yet it will do so against genuine critical principles, which can therefore be commended in these terms :

> ignavum, fucos, pecus a praesepibus arcent.
> *Virg.*[1]

[1] Virgil : *Georgics*, IV. 168.   " they keep out the drones, a slothful herd, from the hives ".

PROLEGOMENA

Preamble

Of what is Peculiar to all metaphysical Knowledge

§ 1

Of the sources of metaphysics.

If a field of knowledge is to be exhibited as a *science*, its differentia, which it has in common with no other science and which is thus *peculiar* to it, must first be capable of being determined exactly; otherwise the boundaries of all the sciences run into one another and none of them can be treated soundly according to its own nature.

This peculiarity, whether it consists in the difference of the *object*, or of the *sources of knowledge*, or of the *kind of knowledge*, or of some if not all of these together, is the basis of the idea of the possible science and of its territory.

First, as regards the *sources* of metaphysical knowledge, it lies in the very concept of metaphysics that they cannot be empirical. Its principles (which comprise not only its fundamental propositions but also its fundamental concepts) must never be taken from experience; for it is not to be physical but metaphysical knowledge, i.e. lying beyond experience. Thus neither outer experience, which provides the source of physics proper, nor inner experience, which provides the basis for empirical psychology, will be the ground of metaphysics. Metaphysics is thus knowledge *a priori*, or out of pure understanding and pure reason.

But there is nothing in this to differentiate metaphysics from pure mathematics; it will therefore have to be called *pure philosophical knowledge*. For the meaning of this term

I refer to Critique of p.R., p. 712 et seq.,[1] where the difference between these two ways of using reason has been
clearly and adequately described.—So much of the sources
of metaphysical knowledge.

§ 2

Of the kind of knowledge that alone can be called
metaphysical.

(a) Of the distinction between synthetic and
analytic judgements in general.

Metaphysical knowledge must contain nothing but
judgements *a priori* ; this is demanded by what is peculiar
to its sources.   But whatever origin judgements may have,
or whatever they may be like as to their logical form, there
is in them a distinction according to content, by virtue of
which they are either merely *explicative* and add nothing
to the content of the knowledge, or *ampliative* and enlarge
the given knowledge ; the former can be called *analytic*
judgements, the latter *synthetic* judgements.

Analytic judgements say nothing in the predicate that
was not already really thought in the concept of the subject,
though not so clearly and with the same consciousness.   If
I say : all bodies are extended, I have not amplified my
concept of body in the least, but only analysed it.   Extension, though not explicitly said of that concept, was already
thought of it before the judgement.   The judgement is
thus analytic.   On the other hand the proposition : some
bodies are heavy contains something in the predicate that
is not really thought in the universal concept of body.   It
thus enlarges my knowledge in that it adds something to

[1] i.e. A712/B740 et seq., The Discipline of Pure Reason in its Dogmatic Employment.   Kant here asks the question whether the method
of reaching apodictical certainty in mathematics is the same as the
method for reaching the same certainty in philosophy, and answers it
by distinguishing philosophical knowledge as knowledge by reason out
of concepts, and mathematical knowledge as knowledge by reason out
of the construction of concepts.   This point is taken up again below,
pp. 21 and 37.

my concept, and hence must be called a synthetic judgement.

(b) The common principle of all analytic
judgements is the principle of contradiction.

All analytic judgements rest wholly on the principle of contradiction, and it is in their nature to be knowledge *a priori*, whether the concepts that serve as matter for them are empirical or not. For because the predicate of an affirmative analytic judgement has already been thought in the concept of the subject, it cannot be denied of the subject without contradiction. Similarly its contrary is necessarily denied of the subject in a negative analytic judgement, also in consequence of the principle of contradiction. This is the case with the propositions: every body is extended, and no body is unextended (simple).

For the same reason all analytic propositions are judgements *a priori*, even though their concepts are empirical, e.g. gold is a yellow metal; for to know this I need no further experience outside my concept of gold, which contained that this body is yellow and metal; for this is what constituted my concept, and I needed to do nothing except analyse it, without looking round elsewhere outside it.

(c) Synthetic judgements need a different principle
from the principle of contradiction.

There are synthetic judgements *a posteriori*, which have an empirical origin; but there are also synthetic judgements which have *a priori* certainty, and have their origin in pure understanding and reason. Both agree in that they can never originate according to the principle of analysis alone, namely the principle of contradiction. They require another quite different principle, although whatever principle they are deduced from, they must always be deduced *in conformity with the principle of contradiction*. For nothing may be contrary to this principle, even though not everything can be deduced from it. I shall first classify the synthetic judgements.

1) *Judgements of experience* [1] are always synthetic. For it would be absurd to ground an analytic judgement on experience, as I do not have to go outside my concept in order to make the judgement, and so have no need of the testimony of experience. That a body is extended is a proposition which holds *a priori*, and not a judgement of experience. For before I proceed to experience I already have in the concept of body all the conditions for my judgement. I have only to extract the predicate from it according to the principle of contradiction, and by so doing can at the same time become conscious of the *necessity* of the judgement—and that is what experience would never teach me.

2) *Mathematical judgements* [2] are all without exception synthetic. This proposition, though incontestably certain and in its consequences very important, seems to have wholly escaped hitherto the notice of the analysers of human reason, indeed to be directly opposed to all their conjectures. For because they found that all the inferences of mathematicians proceed according to the principle of contradiction (which the nature of any apodictical certainty requires), they persuaded themselves that the principles [3] were also known from the principle of contradiction ; in which they made a great mistake. For one can of course have insight into a synthetic proposition according to the principle of contradiction, but only by presupposing another synthetic proposition from which it can be made to follow, never in and by itself.

First of all it has to be noted : that properly mathematical propositions are always judgements *a priori*, and not empirical, because they carry with them necessity,

[1] Part of Section IV of the Introduction to the second edition of the *Critique of Pure Reason*, (B11–12,) is identical, but for a few insignificant differences, with this sub-section (1).

[2] Section V. 1 of the Introduction to the second edition of the *Critique of Pure Reason*, B14–17, is identical, except for a few insignificant differences and a few of substance which are noted, with this sub-section (2).

[3] lit. " fundamental propositions ". See Introduction, p. xxv.

which cannot be taken from experience. But if this be not granted me, very well, I will limit my proposition to *pure mathematics*, the very concept of which carries with it that it does not contain empirical knowledge, but merely pure knowledge *a priori*.

One might indeed think at first that the proposition $7 + 5 = 12$ is a merely analytic proposition, which follows according to the principle of contradiction from the concept of a sum of seven and five. But if we look more closely, we find that the concept of the sum of 7 and 5 contains nothing further than the unification of the two numbers into a single number, and in this we do not in the least think what this single number may be which combines the two. The concept of twelve is in no way already thought by merely thinking this unification of seven and five, and though I analyse my concept of such a possible sum as long as I please, I shall never find the twelve in it. We have to go outside these concepts and with the help of the intuition which corresponds to one of them, our five fingers for instance or (as SEGNER does in his Arithmetic [1]) five points, add to the concept of seven, unit by unit, the five given in intuition. Thus we really amplify our concept by this proposition $7 + 5 = 12$, and add to the first concept a new one which was not thought in it.[2] That is to say, arithmetical propositions are always synthetic, of which we shall be the more clearly aware if we take rather larger numbers. For it is then obvious that however we might turn and twist our concept, we could never find the sum

[1] J. A. Segner : *Elementa Arithmeticae et Geometriae*, Göttingen, 1739 ; German translation, 2nd edition, Halle, 1773.

[2] Instead of this sentence " Thus we really . . . thought in it.", the corresponding section in the *Critique of Pure Reason*, B15-16, reads as follows : " For I first take the number 7, and with the help of the fingers of my hand as intuition for the concept of 5, I add the units, which I previously took together to make up the number 5, one by one to the number 7 in my picture, and thus I see the number 12 arise. In the concept of a sum = $7 + 5$ I have thought that 7 *is to be* added to 5, but not that this sum is equal to the number 12."

by means of mere analysis of our concepts without seeking the aid of intuition.

Nor is any principle of pure geometry analytic. That the straight line between two points is the shortest is a synthetic proposition. For my concept of *straight* contains nothing of quantity but only a quality. The concept of the shortest is therefore wholly an addition, and cannot be drawn by any analysis from the concept of the straight line. Intuition, by means of which alone the synthesis is possible, must therefore be called in here to help.

Some other principles presupposed by geometers are indeed really analytic and rest on the principle of contradiction. But, as identical propositions, they only serve as links in the chain of method and not as principles; for example $a = a$, the whole is equal to itself, or $(a + b) > a$, i.e. the whole is greater than its part. And yet even these propositions, though indeed valid according to concepts alone, are only admitted in mathematics because they can be exhibited in intuition.

What [1] makes us commonly believe that the predicate of such apodictic judgements is already contained in our concept and that the judgement is therefore analytic, is merely the ambiguity of the term. We *are required* to join in thought a certain predicate to a given concept, and this

[1] The original editions of the *Prolegomena* and of the *Critique of Pure Reason* do not make a new paragraph here. Numerous translators and commentators have pointed out that this paragraph (which deals with judgements mistakenly supposed to be analytic) makes nonsense if read as referring to the previous paragraph (which deals with genuinely analytic judgements), but makes sense if read as referring to the next previous paragraph. The appropriate adjustment may be made either by reversing the order of this and the previous paragraph, or preferably by reading the paragraph " Some other principles . . ." as a parenthesis or footnote.

As the end of this paragraph is the point at which the long misplaced section begins, which in its turn includes the point at which the supposed missing section on natural science (p. 22) should have appeared, we must suppose some considerable mix-up here in the manuscript or proof.

necessity is inherent in the concepts themselves. But the question is not what we are *required* to join *in thought* to the given concept, but what we *really think* in it, even if only obscurely. It is then manifest that while the predicate is indeed attached to the concept necessarily, it is so, not immediately,[1] but by means of an intuition which must also be present.

The [2] essential difference of pure *mathematical* knowledge from all other knowledge *a priori* is that it must *never* proceed *from concepts*, but always only by construction of concepts (Critique p. 713).[3] In its propositions pure mathematics must therefore go beyond the concept to what the corresponding intuition contains ; hence its propositions can and should never originate from analysis of concepts, i.e. analytically, and are therefore without exception synthetic.

I cannot refrain from noting the disadvantage that the neglect of this otherwise easy and apparently unimportant observation has brought to philosophy. HUME, when he felt the call, worthy of a philosopher, to cast his eye over the whole field of pure knowledge *a priori*, in which the human understanding presumes to such large possessions, negligently cut off from it a whole, indeed its most considerable, province, namely pure mathematics. He imagined that the nature and so to speak the constitution of this province rested on quite different principles, namely on the principle of contradiction alone ; and although he did not make as formal and universal a classification of propositions as I do here, or use the same names, it was exactly as if he had said : pure mathematics merely contains analytic propositions, but metaphysics contains synthetic propositions *a priori*. Now in this he made a very great

---

[1] *Critique of Pure Reason*, B17 : " not as thought in the concept itself " (see p. 18).

[2] Beginning of misplaced section. See Introduction, p. x.

[3] *Critique of Pure Reason*, A713/B741. For a previous reference to this passage see p. 16.

mistake, which clearly had injurious consequences for his comprehension as a whole. For if he had not done this he would have enlarged his question about the origin of our synthetic judgements far beyond his metaphysical concept of causality, and would have extended it to include the possibility of mathematics *a priori*; for he would have had to take mathematics as also being synthetic. But he would then never have been able to ground his metaphysical propositions on mere experience, because otherwise he would also have submitted the axioms of pure mathematics to experience; and he had too much insight to do this. The good company into which metaphysics would then have been introduced would have saved it from the danger of vile maltreatment, for the blows intended for metaphysics would certainly have also fallen on mathematics, which was not and could not be his intention; and so the sagacious man would have been drawn into considerations which must have been similar to those that now occupy us, but which would have gained immeasurably from his inimitably fine style.

[[3]] *Natural science* [1] (*Physica*) contains in itself synthetic judgements *a priori* as principles. I will only cite a few propositions as examples: the propositions that in all changes in the corporeal world the quantity of matter remains unchanged, or that in all communication of movement action and reaction must always be equal.

---

[1] The original editions continue here with the paragraph " Properly metaphysical judgements . . .". But when incorporating this whole section (§ 2 (c)) into Section IV and V of the Introduction to the second edition of the *Critique*, Kant broke off at the end of § 2 (c) as printed (i.e. before the misplaced section) and completed his Section V with a newly written paragraph on natural science, followed by another short paragraph on metaphysics roughly corresponding to paragraph (4) below. At the ends of § 4 and § 5 below, apparently in allusion to this section, natural science is mentioned in conjunction with mathematics. We therefore conjecture that a paragraph on natural science has been lost here.

We interpolate the relevant paragraph from the *Critique*; presumably the lost paragraph would have been fuller.

Both, it is clear, are not only necessary and *a priori* in origin, but also synthetic. For in the concept of matter I do not think its permanence but only its presence in space by occupying it. Thus I really go beyond the concept of matter in order to add to it *a priori* in thought something which I did not think in it. The proposition is therefore not analytic but synthetic, but yet thought *a priori*, and so are the other propositions of the pure part of natural science.]

[4) [1]] *Properly metaphysical* judgements are without exception synthetic. Judgements *belonging to metaphysics* must be distinguished from properly *metaphysical* judgements. Very many among the former are analytic, but they only form the means to metaphysical judgements which are the whole aim of this science, and which are always synthetic. For if a concept, e.g. that of substance, belongs to metaphysics, judgements which originate in mere analysis of this concept also belong necessarily to metaphysics, e.g. substance is that which only exists as subject etc. By means of several such analytic judgements we try to arrive at the definition of a concept. But as the analysis of a pure concept of the understanding (such as metaphysics contains) does not proceed in any other way than the analysis of all other concepts, empirical included, that do not belong to metaphysics (e.g. air is an elastic fluid, the elasticity of which is not suspended by any known degree of cold), the analytic judgement is not peculiarly metaphysical, even though the concept is. For this science has something special and peculiar to itself in the generation of its cognitions *a priori*, and this generation must therefore be distinguished from what the science has in common with all other knowledge by the understanding ; thus for example the proposition : everything that is substance in things is permanent, is a synthetic and peculiarly metaphysical proposition.

When the concepts *a priori* which constitute the matter of metaphysics and its building-stones have been collected

[1] " 4) " does not appear in the original editions.

according to certain principles, the analysis of these concepts is of great value. It can also be expounded separately from all the synthetic propositions which constitute metaphysics itself, as a distinct part (as it were as *philosophia definitiva*[1]) containing nothing but analytic propositions belonging to metaphysics. For these analyses have in fact no appreciable utility anywhere else than in metaphysics, i.e. with a view to the synthetic propositions that are to be generated out of the concepts *a priori* when they have been analysed.

The conclusion of this paragraph is therefore : that metaphysics has to do properly with synthetic propositions *a priori*, and these alone constitute its end, for which it does indeed require many analyses of its concepts and many analytic judgements, in which the procedure is no different from that in every other kind of knowledge when we merely try to clarify our concepts by analysis. But the *generation* of knowledge *a priori*, both according to intuition and according to concepts, and finally the generation of synthetic propositions *a priori* in philosophical knowledge, constitutes the essential content of metaphysics.[2]

§ 3

Note

to the universal division of judgements into analytic and synthetic.

This division is indispensable in respect of the critique of human understanding, and hence deserves to be *classical* in it ; I do not know of anywhere else where it would be of any appreciable utility. And in this I find the reason why dogmatic philosophers neglected this division, which

---

[1] An example well-known to Kant's contemporaries, the title of which explains the usage of the term, is Fr. Chr. Baumeister's *Philosophia definitiva, h.e. definitiones Philosophicae ex systemate celeb. Wolfii in unum collectae*, Wittenberg, 1733, 3rd edition 1771.

[2] End of misplaced section.

seems to come forward of itself. They were always looking for the sources of metaphysics inside metaphysics itself, instead of outside it in the pure laws of reason in general, and like the illustrious WOLFF or the sagacious BAUM-GARTEN [1] following in his footsteps, could try to find the proof of the principle of sufficient reason, which is manifestly synthetic, in the principle of contradiction. On the other hand I already find a hint of this division in LOCKE's essays on the human understanding. For in the fourth book, third chapter, § 9 et seq., having previously discussed the different ways of connecting representations in judgements [2] with their sources, of which he found one in identity or contradiction [3] (analytic judgements) and the other in the existence of representations in a subject [4] (synthetic judgements), he admits in § 10 that our knowledge (*a priori*) of the latter is very narrow and almost nothing at all. [5] But there is so little that is determined

---

[1] Christian Wolff (1679–1754), the fountain-head of 'the Leibniz-Wolffian philosophy', and his pupil and disciple A. G. Baumgarten (1714–1762) whose Metaphysics, first published in 1739 and repeatedly re-issued, was used for a time by Kant as a text-book for his lectures.

[2] Locke : *Essay*, IV. iii. 7. " The affirmations or negations we make concerning the ideas we have, may, as I have before intimated in general, be reduced to these four sorts, viz., identity, coexistence, relation, and real existence."

[3] IV. iii. 8. " Our knowledge of identity and diversity . . ."

[4] IV. iii. 9. " For our ideas of the species of substances being, as I have showed, nothing but certain collections of simple ideas united in one subject, and so coexisting together, . . ." Here and throughout the *Essay*, Locke uses the term " subject " in the sense in which substance is the subject of predicates, and thus to mean the object perceived ; whereas Kant also, and apparently here, uses " subject " for the perceiving subject.

[5] IV. iii. 10. " This [knowledge of coexistence], how weighty and considerable a part soever of human science, is yet very narrow, and scarce any at all. The reason whereof is, that the simple ideas whereof our complex ideas of substances are made up, are, for the most part, such as carry with them, in their own nature, no visible necessary connection or inconsistency with any other simple ideas, whose coexistence with them we would inform ourselves about."

and reduced to rules in what he says of this kind of know-ledge, that it is not to be wondered at if it prompted no-one, and in particular not even HUME, to consider propositions of this kind. For such universal and yet determinate principles are not easily learnt from others who have only had them floating obscurely before them. One has to come on them first oneself by one's own thinking; after-wards one also finds them elsewhere, where one would certainly not have found them before because the authors did not even know themselves that their own remarks were grounded on such an idea. Those who never think for themselves nevertheless possess the perspicacity to descry everything, after it has been shown to them, in what has already been said, where no-one could see it before.

§ 4

If metaphysics able to assert itself as a science were real ;
if we could say : here is metaphysics, all you have to do
is to learn it, and it will convince you of its truth, irre-
sistibly and immutably ; then this question would be
unnecessary, and the only question that would be left,
more as a test of our sagacity than as a proof of the existence
of the thing itself, would be *how it is possible*, and how reason
should set about attaining it. Now in the case of metaphysics things have not turned out so well for human
reason. There is no single book that one can point to, as
one might hold up a Euclid, and say, this is metaphysics,
here you will find knowledge of a highest being and of a
future world, which is the noblest aim of this science,
proved from principles of pure reason. For although
many propositions can be pointed out to us which are
apodictically certain and have never been disputed, these
are without exception analytic, and concern the materials
and building-stones of metaphysics rather than the enlargement of our knowledge, which is what we are properly
supposed to be aiming at with metaphysics (§ 2 (c)).[2] But
even if you point to synthetic propositions (e.g. the principle
of sufficient reason) which you have never proved out of
mere reason and as was your duty *a priori*, but which are
gladly granted to you, you will still involve yourself, when
you want to use them to your main end, in such inadmis-

[1] It has been suggested that " general " in this heading is to be taken
in the sense of " principal ", and in the heading to § 5 in the sense of
" generalised " (Vaihinger : *Kommentar*, I. 380).

[2] See p. 23. (This reference, under " § 2 (c) ", to matter in the
transposed passage which was originally printed as part of § 4, provides
final justification for restoring the passage to its proper place.)

sible and uncertain assertions that in all ages one meta-physics has contradicted another, either in respect of the assertions themselves or of their proofs, and has thus destroyed its own claim to lasting approbation.   The very attempts to bring such a science into being were without doubt the first cause of the scepticism that arose so early, a way of thinking in which reason acts so violently towards itself that it could never have arisen except in complete despair of satisfaction in respect of reason's most important designs.   For long before nature first began to be ques-tioned methodically, reason alone, which had gained some measure of practice through ordinary experience, was questioned separately, because reason is always present to us but laws of nature ordinarily have to be painfully sought out.   And so metaphysics floated to the top like foam, but in such a way that as soon as the foam that had been drawn had dissolved, more foam immediately appeared on the surface, always to be eagerly collected by some, while others, instead of looking for the cause of the phenomenon in the depths, thought they were showing their wisdom by ridiculing the vain efforts of the former.[1]

Weary therefore of dogmatism that teaches us nothing, and equally of scepticism that promises us nothing at all, not even to rest in permitted ignorance ; challenged by the importance of the knowledge that we need, and made suspicious by long experience with regard to all the know-ledge that we believe we possess, or that offers itself to us under the title of pure reason—we only have one critical question left, by answering which we can regulate our future conduct : *is metaphysics possible at all*? But this question must not be answered by sceptical objections against particular assertions of a real metaphysics (for at present we do not yet allow the validity of any), but out of the concept, which is now only *problematic*, of such a science.

In the *Critique of Pure Reason* I went to work with regard

[1] Here followed the misplaced section of § 2.

to this question synthetically, namely by enquiring within pure reason itself, and trying to determine in this source itself, according to principles, both the elements and the laws of its pure employment. This task is difficult and demands a reader resolved to think himself gradually into a system which is grounded in nothing regarded as given except reason itself, and thus tries to develop knowledge out of its original seeds without seeking the support of any fact. *Prolegomena* on the contrary ought to be preliminary exercises ; they ought rather to indicate what has to be done in order to bring a science into reality, if it be possible, than to expound the science itself. They must look for support to something that is already known to be reliable, from which one can confidently set out and ascend to the sources which are not yet known, and which, when discovered, will not only explain what we knew already, but will also exhibit a large extent of knowledge which springs exclusively from these same sources. As regards method, the procedure of prolegomena, and especially of those that are to be the preparation for a future metaphysics, will therefore be *analytic*.

It is fortunately the case that, although we cannot assume that metaphysics as a science is *real*, we can confidently say that certain pure synthetic knowledge *a priori* is real and given, namely *pure mathematics* and *pure natural science* ; for both contain propositions which are everywhere recognised, partly as apodictically certain by mere reason, partly by universal agreement from experience, and yet as independent of experience. We have therefore some, at least *incontested*, synthetic knowledge *a priori*, and do not have to ask whether such knowledge is possible (for it is real), but only *how it is possible*, in order to be able to deduce from the principle of the possibility of the given knowledge the possibility of all other synthetic knowledge *a priori*.

GENERAL QUESTION
HOW IS KNOWLEDGE OUT OF PURE REASON POSSIBLE?

§ 5

We have seen above the vast difference between analytic and synthetic judgements. The possibility of analytic propositions could be conceived very easily; for it is grounded solely on the principle of contradiction. The possibility of synthetic propositions *a posteriori*, i.e. of propositions that are drawn from experience, also needs no special explanation; for experience itself is nothing other than a continual joining together (synthesis) of perceptions. Thus we are only left with synthetic propositions *a priori*, the possibility of which must be looked for or enquired into, because it must rest on principles other than the principle of contradiction.

But here we cannot rightly start by looking for the *possibility* of such propositions, i.e. by asking whether they are possible. For there are plenty of them, really given with undisputed certainty, and as the method which we are now following is to be analytic, we shall start from this : that such synthetic but pure knowledge by reason is real. But then we still have to *enquire* into the ground of this possibility, and ask *how* this knowledge is possible, so as to put ourselves in a position to determine, from the principles of its possibility, the conditions of its employment and the extent and boundaries of the same. Expressed with scholastic precision, the proper problem, on which everything depends, is therefore :

How are synthetic propositions a priori possible ?

I have expressed this problem above rather differently, for the sake of popularity, namely as a question about knowledge out of pure reason, which I could well do on this occasion without prejudicing the desired insight, because, as we have to do here solely with metaphysics and its sources, the reader will, I hope, after the foregoing remarks, always remember : that when we speak here of knowledge out of pure reason, it is never a question of analytic but solely of synthetic knowledge.*

Whether metaphysics is to stand or fall, and thus its existence, now entirely depends on the solving of this problem. A man may propound his assertions in metaphysics as plausibly as he will, heaping conclusions on conclusions to suffocation ; if he has not first been able to answer this question satisfactorily, I have the right to say : this is all vain groundless philosophy and false wisdom. You speak through pure reason, and presume as it were to create cognitions *a priori*, not merely by analysing given concepts but by giving out that you are making new connections, which do not rest on the principle of contradiction, and you imagine you have insight into them independently of all experience ; how do you arrive at all this and how will you justify such pretensions ? You cannot be permitted to appeal to the consent of common sense,[1] for this is a witness whose reputation only rests on public rumour.

---

* In consequence of the gradual advance of knowledge it is inevitable that certain expressions that have become classical and have been in use since the childhood of science, will be found inadequate and inappropriate, and that a certain new and more suitable usage will run into some danger of being confused with the old. Analytic method, in so far as it is opposed to the synthetic method, is something quite different from an aggregate of analytic propositions. It means that one starts from what is being looked for as if it were given, and ascends to the conditions under which alone it is possible. In this method one often uses nothing but synthetic propositions, as in the example of mathematical analysis, and it might be better to call it the *regressive* method, in distinction from the synthetic or *progressive* method. The name analytic also occurs as a principal part of logic, and there it is the logic of truth and is opposed to dialectic, without considering specifically whether the cognitions that belong to it are analytic or synthetic.

---

[1] Here lit. " general human reason ". Cf. p. 9.

Quodcunque ostendis mihi sic, incredulus odi.
Horat.[1]

Indispensable as it is to answer this question, it is equally difficult to do so, and although the principal reason why an answer was not attempted long ago is that it never even occurred to anyone that such a question could be asked, a second reason is that a satisfactory answer to this one question demands much deeper, more persistent and painstaking reflection than the most prolix metaphysical work that ever promised immortality to its author on its first appearance. Every discerning reader who carefully thinks over what this problem demands will be frightened at first by its difficulty, and will hold it to be insoluble, and if it were not that there really are such synthetic cognitions *a priori*, hold it to be wholly impossible. This is what really happened to DAVID HUME, although he did not represent the question to himself in anything like such universality as has been done here and must be done, if the answer is to be decisive for the whole of metaphysics. For how is it possible, said the sagacious man, that if a concept is given to me, I can go beyond it and connect with it another concept that is not contained in it, and connect it as if it belonged *necessarily* to the first concept? Only experience can provide us with such connections (so he argued from this difficulty, taking it for an impossibility), and all this supposed necessity, or, what is the same, this supposed knowledge *a priori*, is nothing but a long-standing habit of finding something to be true, and hence of taking subjective necessity to be objective.

If the reader complains about the toil and trouble that I am going to give him in solving this problem, he only has to make the attempt to solve it in an easier way himself. Perhaps he will then feel himself obliged to the man who has taken over for him a task of such deep research, and

[1] Horace: *Epist.* II. 3. 188. " Whatever you show me thus, I hate and do not believe."

will rather show some surprise that, considering the nature of the matter, it has still been possible to make the solution as easy as it is. It has cost the labour of many years to solve this problem in its full universality (in the sense in which mathematicians take this word, namely covering all cases), and finally also to be able to present it as the reader will find it here, in analytic form.

All metaphysicians are therefore solemnly and legally suspended from their business until they have satisfactorily answered the question : *How are synthetic cognitions a priori possible?* For in this answer alone are to be found the credentials which they must show if they have anything to offer us in the name of pure reason ; without these they can only expect to be turned away by all reasonable men, who have so often been deceived, without any further enquiry into what they are offering.

If on the other hand they want to carry on their business not as *science* but as an *art* of wholesome persuasions suitable for ordinary common sense, they cannot in fairness be prevented from following this trade. They will then speak the modest language of rational belief, they will admit that they are not even allowed to *guess*, let alone to *know*, anything about what lies beyond the bounds of all possible experience, but only to *assume* something (not for speculative use, for they must renounce this, but solely for practical use) that is possible and even indispensable in life for the guidance of the understanding and the will. Only thus will they deserve the name of useful and wise men, the more so, the more they renounce the name of metaphysicians ; for metaphysicians aim to be speculative philosophers and since stale probabilities cannot be the target when it is a question of judgements *a priori* (for what is said to be known *a priori* is thereby announced as necessary), they cannot be permitted to play with guesses. What they assert must be science, otherwise it is nothing at all.

It can be said that the whole transcendental philosophy

which necessarily precedes all metaphysics is itself nothing other than merely the complete solution of the question proposed here, only in systematic order and in full detail, and that until now we have had no transcendental philosophy ; for what bears its name is properly a part of metaphysics ; but the former science has first to settle the possibility of the latter, and must therefore precede all metaphysics. Merely to answer one single question adequately, we need a whole science, a science deprived of all assistance from others and in itself wholly new ; it is not therefore to be wondered at if the solution to this question is joined with trouble and difficulty and even with some obscurity.

In now proceeding to this solution, according to the analytic method, in which we presuppose that such cognitions out of pure reason are real, we can appeal to only two *sciences* of theoretical knowledge (with which alone we are here concerned), namely *pure mathematics* and *pure natural science*, for only these can represent objects to us in intuition, and if a cognition *a priori* should occur in them, show us *in concreto* its truth, or its agreement with the object, i.e. show us its *reality*, from which we could then go on in the analytic way to the ground of its possibility. This makes things much easier, in that universal considerations, as well as being applied to facts, also start from them, instead of, as in the synthetic procedure, having to be deduced wholly *in abstracto* out of concepts.

In order to ascend from these kinds of pure knowledge *a priori*, which are both real and grounded, to a possible kind of knowledge which we are seeking, namely to metaphysics as science, we must include under our main question that which gives rise to metaphysics—that *a priori* knowledge merely naturally given, though not above suspicion with regard to its truth, which forms the ground of that science, that knowledge, the elaboration of which without any critical enquiry into its possibility is usually called metaphysics, in a word the natural disposition to such a science.

The main transcendental question will therefore be divided into four other questions and answered in stages.

1) *How is pure mathematics possible?*
2) *How is pure natural science possible?*
3) *How is metaphysics possible in general?*
4) *How is metaphysics possible as a science?*

It can be seen that although the solution of these problems is mainly designed to exhibit the essential content of the Critique, it also has something peculiar to itself which is worth attention for its own sake, namely that we are looking for the sources of given sciences in reason itself, and in so doing investigating and measuring out for reason, by means of the deed itself, its power of knowing anything *a priori*. These sciences themselves then profit by this, if not in respect of their content, yet as concerns their correct employment, and in throwing light on a higher question about their common origin give occasion at the same time for their own nature to be more clearly revealed.

First Part

HOW IS PURE MATHEMATICS POSSIBLE ?

§ 6

Here is a great and proved field of knowledge, which is already of admirable compass and for the future promises unbounded extension, which carries with it thoroughly apodictic certainty, i.e. absolute necessity, hence rests on no grounds of experience, is a pure product of reason, and moreover is thoroughly synthetic : " how is it possible for human reason to bring into being such knowledge wholly *a priori* ? " Does not this faculty, which is not based on experience and cannot be, presuppose some *a priori* ground of knowledge, which lies deeply hidden, but which might reveal itself through these its effects, if their first beginnings were only diligently tracked down ?

§ 7

But we find that all mathematical knowledge has this peculiarity, that it must first exhibit its concept *in intuition*, and do so *a priori*, in an intuition that is not empirical but pure ; without this means mathematics cannot make a single step. Hence its judgements are always *intuitive*, instead of which philosophy has to be satisfied with *discursive* judgements *out of mere concepts*, and may illustrate its apodictic doctrines through intuition but can never deduce them from it. This observation with regard to the nature of mathematics gives us a lead to the first and highest condition of its possibility : namely, it must have as its ground some *pure intuition* in which it can represent all its concepts *in concreto* and yet *a priori*, or, as it is called, can *construct* them *. If we can discover this pure intuition and the possibility of it, we shall thence easily be able to explain how synthetic propositions *a priori* are possible in pure mathematics, and also how this science itself is possible ; for as empirical intuition makes it possible without difficulty for the concept which we make for ourselves of an object of intuition to be amplified synthetically in experience by new predicates which intuition itself offers, so pure intuition will do the same, only with this difference : that in the latter case the synthetic judgement will be *a priori* certain and apodictic, but in the former case only *a posteriori* and empirically certain, because the former only contains what is met with in chance empirical intuition, whereas the latter will contain what must necessarily be met with in pure intuition, in that as intuition *a priori* it is inseparably joined with the concept *before all experience* or particular perception.

§ 8

But with this step the difficulty seems rather to grow than to decrease. For now the question runs : *how is it possible to intuit anything a priori?* Intuition is a representation, such as would depend directly on the presence of the object. Hence it seems impossible to intuit anything *a priori originally*, because the intuition would then have to take place without any object being present, either previously or now, to which it could refer, and so could not be an intuition. Concepts are indeed of such a nature that we can very well make some of them for ourselves *a priori*, without ourselves standing in any immediate relation to the object ; namely the concepts that only contain the thought of an object in general, e.g. the concepts of quantity, cause etc. But even these, to provide them with meaning and sense, still require a certain use *in concreto*, i.e. application to some

* See Critique p. 713 [1].

[1] i.e. A713/B741. For previous references to this passage, see pp. 16 and 21.

intuition through which an object of these concepts is given to us. But how can *intuition* of the object precede the object itself?

§ 9

If our intuition had to be of such a nature that it represented things *as they are in themselves,* no intuition *a priori* would ever take place and intuition would be empirical every time. For I can only know what is contained in the object in itself if the object is present and given to me. Of course it is then still inconceivable how the intuition of a thing that is present should make me know it as it is in itself, for its properties cannot migrate into my faculty of representation; but even granting this possibility, such an intuition would not take place *a priori,* i.e. before the object was presented to me; for without its presence no ground for the reference to it of my representation is conceivable, unless it rested on inspiration. There is thus only one way in which it is possible for my intuition to precede the reality of the object and take place as knowledge *a priori, namely if it contains nothing else than the form of sensibility which in me as subject precedes all real impressions through which I am affected by objects.* That objects of the senses can only be intuited in accordance with this form of sensibility is something that I can know *a priori.* From this it follows: that propositions which concern merely this form of sensible intuition will be possible and valid for objects of the senses; equally the converse, that intuitions which are possible *a priori,* can never concern any other things than objects of our senses.

§ 10

Thus it is only through the form of sensible intuition that we can intuit things *a priori,* but through it we can only know objects as they *appear* to us (to our senses), not as they may be in themselves; and this presupposition is absolutely necessary if synthetic propositions *a priori* are to be granted as possible, or should we really encounter them,

38

if their possibility is to be conceived and determined in advance.

Now space and time are the two intuitions on which pure mathematics grounds all its cognitions and judgements that present themselves as at once apodictic and necessary ; for mathematics must first exhibit all its concepts in intuition, and pure mathematics exhibit them in pure intuition, i.e. construct them. Without pure intuition (as mathematics cannot proceed analytically, namely by analysis of concepts, but only synthetically) it is impossible for pure mathematics to make a single step, since it is in pure intuition alone that the material for synthetic judgements *a priori* can be given. Geometry is grounded on the pure intuition of space. Arithmetic forms its own concepts of numbers by successive addition of units in time ; and pure mechanics especially can only form its concepts of motion by means of the representation of time. But both representations are merely intuitions ; for if everything empirical, namely what belongs to sensation, is taken away from the empirical intuitions of bodies and their changes (motion), space and time are still left. These are therefore pure intuitions, which are the ground *a priori* of the empirical intuitions, and hence can never be taken away themselves, but prove, precisely by being pure intuitions *a priori*, that they are mere forms of our sensibility which must precede all empirical intuition, i.e. perception of real objects, and in conformity with which objects can be known *a priori*, though indeed only as they appear to us.

§ 11

The problem of the present section is thus solved. Pure mathematics, as synthetic knowledge *a priori*, is only possible because it bears on none other than mere objects of the senses, the empirical intuition of which is grounded *a priori* in a pure intuition (of space and time), and can be so grounded because the pure intuition is nothing but the mere form of sensibility which precedes the real appear-

ance of objects, in that only through it are they in fact
made possible.   But yet this faculty of intuiting *a priori* is
not concerned with the matter of the appearance, i.e. what
is sensation in it, for this is what constitutes the empirical,
but only with the form of the appearance, space and time.
If anyone were to have the slightest doubt that both are
not determinations of things in themselves but only mere
determinations of their relation to sensibility, I should like
to know how it could be found possible to know *a priori*
and thus prior to all acquaintance with things, namely
before they are given to us, what their intuition must be
like, which is the case here with space and time.   But this
is quite conceivable as soon as both count as nothing more
than formal conditions of our sensibility, and objects merely
as appearances, for then the form of the appearance, i.e.
the pure intuition, can certainly be represented out of ourselves, i.e. *a priori*.

§ 12

To add something by way of elucidation and confirmation, we need only look at the usual and absolutely necessary procedure of geometers.   All proofs of the complete
congruence of two given figures (when one can be replaced
at all points by the other) finally come to this, that they
coincide with each other ; which is obviously nothing other
than a synthetic proposition resting on immediate intuition.
This intuition must be given pure and *a priori*, otherwise
the proposition could not hold as apodictically certain, but
would only have empirical certainty.   It would only mean :
it is always observed thus and the proposition holds only as
far as our perception has extended up to now.   That complete space (which is not itself the boundary of another
space) has three dimensions, and that space in general cannot have more, is built on the proposition that not more
than three lines can intersect at right angles in a point.
This proposition cannot be shown from concepts, but rests
immediately on intuition, and indeed, because it is apodic-

tically certain, on pure intuition *a priori*. That we can require that a line shall be drawn to infinity (*in indefinitum*) or a series of changes (e.g. spaces passed through in movement) continued to infinity, presupposes a representation of space and time which, in respect of not being in itself bounded by anything, can only attach to intuition ; for it could never be inferred from concepts. Thus mathematics is really grounded in pure intuitions *a priori*, which make possible its synthetic propositions that hold apodictically, and hence our transcendental deduction of the concepts of space and time also explains the possibility of a pure mathematics. Without such a deduction and without our accepting that " everything which may be given to our senses (to outer senses in space and to inner sense in time) is only intuited by us as it appears to us, not as it is in itself ", we could, it is true, grant the possibility of a pure mathematics, but we could in no way gain insight into it.

§ 13

Those who cannot get away from the concept that space and time are real qualities attached to things in themselves, may exercise their sagacity on the following paradox, and when they have tried in vain to solve it, may suspect, free from prejudices at least for a few moments, that the reduction of space and time to mere forms of our sensible intuition may perhaps have some ground.

If two things are completely the same in all points that can be known at all about each separately (in all determinations belonging to quantity and quality), it must follow that each can be replaced by the other in all cases and in all respects, without the exchange causing the slightest recognisable difference. This is in fact the case with plane figures in geometry ; but various spherical figures show, notwithstanding this complete inner agreement, an outer relation such that one cannot be replaced by the other. For example two spherical triangles on opposite hemispheres which have an arc of the equator as their common base can be completely equal, in respect of sides as well as angles, so that nothing is found in either, when it is described alone and completely, which does not also appear in the description of the other, and yet one cannot be put in the place of the other (on the opposite hemisphere). Here then is an *inner* difference between the two triangles which no understanding can show to be inner and which only reveals itself through the outer relation in space.   But I will quote more usual cases which can be taken from ordinary life.

What can be more like my hand or my ear, and more equal in all points, than its image in the mirror? And yet I cannot put such a hand as is seen in the mirror in the place of its original : for if the original was a right hand, the hand in the mirror is a left hand, and the image of the right ear is a left ear, which could never serve as a substitute for the other. Here are no inner differences that any understanding could think ; and yet the differences are inner as far as the senses tell us, for the left hand cannot be enclosed in the same boundaries as the right (they cannot be congruent) notwithstanding all their mutual equality and similarity ; the glove of the one hand cannot be used on the other. What is the solution? These objects are not representations of the things as they are in themselves and as a pure [1] understanding would know them, but sensible intuitions, i.e. appearances, the possibility of which rests on the relation of certain things, unknown in themselves, to something else, namely our sensibility. Now of this sensibility space is the form of outer intuition, and the inner determination of any space is only possible by determining its outer relation to space as a whole of which it is a part (the relation to outer sense), i.e. the part is only possible through the whole, which is never the case with things in themselves as objects of bare

[1] Kant distinguishes the use of ' pure ' here from its usual use in ' pure intuition ', etc., by putting the Latin form *pur* instead of the usual *rein*. He also writes ' bare ' (*bloss*) nine lines below.

understanding, but can well be with mere appearances. Hence we cannot make the difference between similar and equal but yet incongruent things (e.g. spirals winding opposite ways [1]) intelligible by any single concept, but only by their relation to the right and the left hand, which bears immediately on intuition.

Note I

Pure mathematics, and in particular pure geometry, can only have objective reality under the condition that it bears merely on objects of the senses, in respect of which this principle holds good : that our sensible representation is in no way a representation of things in themselves, but only of the way they appear to us. From this it follows that the propositions of geometry are not determinations of a mere creature of our poetic fantasy which could not be reliably referred to real objects, but that they hold necessarily of space and hence also of everything that may be encountered in space, because space is nothing other than the form of all outer appearances under which alone objects of the senses can be given to us. Sensibility, the form of which is the ground of geometry, is that on which the possibility of outer appearances rests ; hence these can never contain anything other than what geometry prescribes to them. It would be quite different if the senses had to represent objects as they are in themselves. For then it would not follow at all from the representation of space which with all its various properties the geometer has as ground *a priori* that all this, together with what is inferred from it, would have to be just so in nature. The space of the geometer would be held to be mere fiction and would be allowed no objective validity ; because it cannot be seen how things must agree necessarily with the picture that we make of them by ourselves and in advance.

[1] All the previous translators have noted the memorable rendering of this phrase in Richardson's translation (London, 1819, p. 50) : " for instance, snails rolled up contrary to all sense ".

But if this picture, or rather this formal intuition, is the essential property of our sensibility, by means of which alone objects are given to us, and if this sensibility does not represent things in themselves but only their appearances, it is then quite easy to conceive and at the same time is proved irrefutably : that all outer objects of the world of our senses must necessarily agree in all exactitude with the propositions of geometry, because it is sensibility itself that first makes these objects possible as mere appearances, by its form of outer intuition (space) with which the geometer is concerned. It will always remain a remarkable phenomenon in the history of philosophy that there was a time when even mathematicians who were also philosophers began to doubt, not indeed the correctness of their geometrical propositions in so far as they merely concern space, but the objective validity and application to nature of this concept itself and of all geometrical determinations of it. They were anxious whether a line in nature might not consist of physical points and true space in the object, of simple parts, although the space that the geometer thinks about can in no way consist of these. They did not recognise that it is this space in thought which itself makes possible physical space, i.e. the extension of matter ; that it is not a quality of things in themselves but only a form of our faculty of sensible representation ; that all objects in space are mere appearances, i.e. not things in themselves but representations of our sensible intuition ; and that space, as the geometer thinks it, being precisely the form of sensible intuition which we find in ourselves *a priori* and which contains the ground of the possibility of all outer appearances (as to their form), it must agree necessarily and in the most precise way with the propositions of the geometer, which he draws from no fictitious concept, but from the subjective foundation of all outer appearances, namely sensibility itself. In this and no other way can the geometer be secured as to the undoubted objective reality of his propositions against all the chicaneries of a shallow metaphysics, however strange this may seem to a metaphysics which does not go back to the sources of its concepts.

Note II [1]

Everything that is to be given to us as an object must be given to us in intuition. But all our intuition happens only by means of the senses ; the understanding intuits nothing but only reflects. As the senses, according to what has now been demonstrated, never and in no single instance enable us to know things in themselves, but only their appearances, and as these are mere representations of sensibility, " all bodies, together with the space in which they are, must be held to be nothing but mere representations in us, and exist nowhere else than merely in our thoughts ". Now is this not manifest idealism ?

Idealism consists in the assertion that there are none other than thinking beings ; the other things which we believe we perceive in intuition are only representations in the thinking beings, to which in fact no object outside the latter corresponds. I say on the contrary : things are given to us as objects of our senses situated outside us, but of what they may be in themselves we know nothing ; we only know their appearances, i.e. the representations that they effect in us when they affect our senses. Consequently I do indeed admit that there are bodies outside us, i.e. things which, although wholly unknown to us as to what they may be in themselves, we know through the representations which their influence on our sensibility provides for us, and to which we give the name of bodies. This word therefore merely means the appearance of that for us unknown but none the less real object. Can this be called idealism ? It is the very opposite of it.

That it can be said of many of the predicates of outer

---

[1] The matter of Notes II and III is in the main identical with part of the reply to the Göttingen review (*Specimen of a judgement . . .*, p. 143, below).

things, without detriment to their real existence, that they belong not to these things in themselves but only to their appearances and have no existence of their own outside our representations, is something that was generally accepted and admitted long before LOCKE's time, but more so afterwards. To these predicates belong heat, colour, taste, etc. But that I for weighty reasons also count as mere appearances, in addition to these, the remaining qualities of bodies which are called *primariae*, extension, place, and space in general with all that depends on it (impenetrability or materiality, shape, etc.) is something against which not the slightest ground of inadmissibility can be adduced. A man who will not allow colours to be attached to the object in itself as qualities, but only to the sense of sight as modifications, cannot be called an idealist for that; equally little can my doctrine be called idealistic merely because I find that more of, *indeed all, the qualities that make up the intuition of a body* belong merely to its appearance; for the existence of the thing that appears is not thereby cancelled, as with real idealism, but it is only shown that we cannot know it at all through the senses as it is in itself.

I should be glad to know what my assertions would have to be like in order not to contain idealism. Doubtless I should have to say: that the representation of space is not only perfectly in conformity with the relation of our sensibility to the objects, for that is what I have said, but also that it is completely like the object; an assertion with which I can connect as little sense as with the assertion that the sensation of red is similar to the property of the vermilion which excites this sensation in me.

Note III

From this an easily foreseeable but vain objection can now be very easily refuted: " namely that by the ideality of space and time the whole world of the senses would be turned into nothing but illusion ". After all philosophical insight into the nature of sensible knowledge had first been spoiled by making sensibility merely into a confused kind of representation, according to which we still know things as they are but without having the power to bring everything in this our representation clearly to consciousness ; whereas on the contrary we have proved that sensibility does not consist in this logical difference of clarity or obscurity but in the genetic difference of the origin of knowledge itself, because sensible knowledge does not represent things as they are but only the way in which they affect our senses, and thus that appearances merely, not the things themselves, are given by it to the understanding for reflection : after this necessary correction an objection arising out of unforgivable and almost deliberate misunderstanding is still raised, as if my doctrine turned all the things of the world of the senses into nothing but illusion.

When appearance is given to us we are still quite free as to how we shall judge the matter from it. The former, namely the appearance, rested on the senses, but this judgement rests on the understanding, and the only question is whether there is truth in the determination of the object or not. But the difference between truth and dreams is not decided by the nature of the representations that we refer to objects, for they are the same in both, but by the connection of these representations according to the rules that determine the combination of them in the concept of an object, and how far they can or cannot stand together in an experience. And it is not the fault of the appearances if our knowledge takes illusion for truth, i.e. if intuition, through which an object is given to us, is taken for the concept of the object or even for the concept of its existence which only the understanding can think. The course of the planets is represented to us by the senses as being now forward now backward, and herein is neither falsehood nor truth, because so long as we concede that this is as yet only appearance, no judgement is made about the objective nature of their motion.   But because, if the understanding does not take good care to prevent this subjective manner of representation from being taken for objective, a false judgement can easily arise, we say : they seem to go back-wards ; but the seeming [1] is not to be accounted to the senses but to the understanding, to which alone it belongs to make an objective judgement out of the appearance.

In this way, even if we do not reflect at all on the origin of our representations, and connect our intuitions of the senses, whatever they may contain, in an experience in space and time according to rules of the combination of all knowledge, deceptive illusion or truth can still arise, according as we are negligent or careful ; that is solely a matter of the use of sensible representations in the under-standing, not of their origin.   Equally, if I hold all repre-sentations of the senses together with their form, namely space and time, to be nothing but appearances, and space and time to be a mere form of sensibility which is not found outside it in the objects, and I use these same representa-tions only in reference to possible experience :   there is neither the slightest inducement to error nor an illusion in my holding them to be mere appearances ; for they can still be combined correctly in experience according to rules of truth.   In this way all the propositions of geometry are valid for space as well as for all objects of the senses and in respect of all possible experience, whether I regard space as a mere form of sensibility or as something attached to the things themselves ; although in the first case alone can I conceive how it is possible to know those propositions *a priori* of all objects of outer intuition ; apart from this, in respect of all possible experience everything remains as if I had never undertaken this defection from the common opinion.

But if I venture to take my concepts of space and time beyond all possible experience, which is unavoidable if I

[1] The word here translated " seeming " (" *Schein* ") also carries the meaning " illusion ", by which it is elsewhere translated.

give them out to be qualities attached to things in themselves (for what should prevent me then from letting them still be valid for these same things, whether my senses were arranged differently and were suited to them or not?), an important error can arise which rests on an illusion. That which, as a condition of the intuition of things, was dependent merely on my subject and was certainly valid for all objects of the senses and for all possible experience, I would have given out to be universally valid because I referred space and time to things in themselves and did not limit them to conditions of experience.

My doctrine of the ideality of space and time, therefore, so far from making the whole world of the senses into mere illusion, is rather the only means of securing the application to real objects of one of the most important kinds of knowledge, namely that which mathematics expounds *a priori*, and of preventing it from being held to be mere illusion, because without this observation it would be quite impossible to decide whether the intuitions of space and time, which we take from no experience and which yet lie in our representation *a priori*, were not mere chimeras of the brain made by us to which no object corresponds, at least not adequately, and thus geometry itself a mere illusion; whereas on the contrary, just because all objects of the world of the senses are mere appearances, we have been able to show the indisputable validity of geometry in respect of them.

Secondly, these my principles, so far from turning the representations of the senses from the truth of experience into mere illusion because they make them into appearances, are rather the only means of avoiding the transcendental illusion, by which metaphysics has always been deceived and has been misled into childish efforts to snatch at soap-bubbles, because appearances, which are mere representations, were taken for things in themselves, from which followed all those remarkable performances of the antinomy of reason, which I shall mention later and which are cancelled by this single observation : that appearance brings forth truth so long as it is used in experience, but as soon as it goes beyond the boundary of experience and becomes transcendent, brings forth nothing but illusion.

As I leave their reality to things that we represent to ourselves through the senses and only limit our sensible intuition of these things in this, that in no instance, not even in the pure intuitions of space and time, does it represent anything more than mere appearance of these things, never their nature in themselves, this is no thorough-going illusion fictitiously attributed by me to nature, and my protestation against all imputation of idealism is so conclusive and clear that it would seem superfluous if there were not unappointed judges who, wanting to have an old name for every deviation from their perverse though common opinion and never judging the spirit of philo-sophical nomenclature but merely clinging to the letter, were ready to put their own error in the place of well-deter-mined concepts, and thereby to twist and deform them. For the fact that I myself gave to this my theory the name of transcendental idealism cannot justify anybody in con-fusing it with the empirical idealism of DESCARTES (although this was only a problem, the insolubility of which gave everyone the liberty, in DESCARTES' opinion, to deny the existence of the corporeal world, because it could never be satisfactorily answered), or with the mystical and visionary idealism of BERKELEY (against which and other similar chimeras of the brain our Critique on the contrary contains the proper antidote). For this idealism, so-called by me, did not concern the existence of things (to doubt which properly constitutes idealism in its accepted mean-ing), for it has never entered my mind to doubt this, but only the sensible representation of things, to which space and time first and foremost belong ; and of these, as in general of all *appearances*, I have only shown : that they are not things (but mere kinds of representation) and not determinations belonging to things in themselves. But the word transcendental, which for me never means a reference of our knowledge to things, but only to our *faculty of knowing*, was intended to prevent this misinterpretation. But rather than that it should cause any more, I prefer to take this name back and will have it called critical idealism.   But if it is indeed an objectionable idealism to turn real things (not appearances) into mere representations, by what name should that be called which on the contrary makes mere representations into things ?   I think it could be called *dreaming* idealism, to distinguish it from the former, which may be called *visionary* idealism, both of which were to have been held off by my formerly so-called transcendental, better *critical* idealism.

Second Part

HOW IS PURE NATURAL SCIENCE POSSIBLE ?

§ 14

Nature is the *existence* of things, considered as existence determined according to universal laws. If nature meant the existence of things *in themselves*, we should never be able to know them, neither *a priori* nor *a posteriori*. Not *a priori*, for how are we to know what may belong to things in themselves, as this can never happen by analysis of our concepts (analytic propositions) since I do not want to know what is contained in my concept of a thing (for that belongs to its logical being) but what is added to this concept in the reality of the thing and what determines the thing itself in its existence outside my concept. My understanding, with the conditions under which alone it can connect the determinations of things in their existence, prescribes no rules to the things themselves ; they do not conform to my understanding, but my understanding would have to conform to them ; they would therefore have to be given to me previously, for me to take these determinations from them, but then they would not be known *a priori*.

A posteriori it would also be impossible for me to have such knowledge of the nature of things in themselves. For if experience is to teach me *laws* to which the existence of things is subject, these laws, in so far as they concerned things in themselves, would also have to apply *necessarily* to them outside my experience. Now experience does indeed teach me what exists and what it is like, but never that it must necessarily be so and not otherwise. Therefore it can never teach me the nature of things in themselves.

§ 15

We are none the less really in possession of pure natural science, in which laws to which nature is subject are propounded *a priori* and with all that necessity which is required for apodictical propositions. Here I need only call to witness that propaedeutic to natural knowledge which under the title of general natural science precedes all physics (which is grounded on empirical principles). In it we find mathematics applied to appearances, and also merely discursive [1] principles (out of concepts) which make up the philosophical part of pure knowledge of nature. But there are also several things in it which are not wholly pure and independent of sources in experience : such as the concept of *motion*, of *impenetrability* (on which the empirical concept of matter rests), of *inertia* and others, which prevent it from being called quite pure natural science ; furthermore it only bears on the objects of the outer senses and therefore does not form an example of a general natural science in the strict meaning, for that must bring nature in general under universal laws, whether nature concerns the object of the outer senses or of inner sense (the object of physics as well as psychology). But there are several among the principles of this general physics which really have the universality that we demand, such as the proposition : *that substance remains* and is permanent, that *everything that happens is* always previously *determined* according to constant laws *by a cause*, etc. These really are universal laws of nature which subsist wholly *a priori*. Thus there is in fact pure natural science and the question now is : *how is it possible ?*

§ 16

The word *nature* takes on another meaning, namely one which determines the *object*, whereas in the above meaning it only indicated the *conformity to law* of the determinations

---

[1] i.e. not, like mathematics, intuitive. See p. 36.

of the existence of things in general.   Nature considered *materialiter* is the *totality of all objects of experience.*   We are only concerned here with experience, for otherwise things that can never be objects of an experience, if they were to be known according to their nature, would drive us to concepts the meaning of which could never be given *in concreto* (in any example of a possible experience).   The concepts which we should thus have to make of the nature of these things would be nothing but concepts the reality of which, that is, whether they really refer to objects or are merely figments of thought, could never be decided. Knowledge of what cannot be an object of experience would be hyperphysical, and here we are not concerned with such knowledge but with knowledge of nature, the reality of which can be confirmed by experience, even though it is *a priori* possible and precedes all experience.

§ 17

The *formal* in nature in this narrower meaning is thus the conformity to law of all objects of experience, and, in so far as they are known *a priori*, their *necessary* conformity to law.   But it has just been shown : that the laws of nature can never be known *a priori* of objects in so far as they are considered not with reference to possible experience but as things in themselves.   But we are not concerned here with things in themselves (the properties of which we leave out of account) but only with things as objects of a possible experience, and the totality of these things is properly what we here call nature.   And now I ask whether, when the possibility of knowledge of nature *a priori* is in question, it is better to arrange the problem thus : how in general is it possible to know *a priori* the necessary conformity to law *of things* as objects of experience, or : how in general is it possible to know *a priori* the necessary conformity to law *of experience* itself in respect of all its objects ?

Looked at in the light of day the solution of the question will come to exactly the same in respect of pure knowledge of nature (which is properly the point of the question) whether it is represented in the one way or in the other. For the subjective laws under which alone knowledge of things by experience is possible also hold good of these things as objects of a possible experience (but not of course of them as things in themselves, which are not under consideration here). It is all one whether I say : without the law that when an event is perceived it is always referred to something preceding it on which it follows according to a universal rule, a judgement of perception can never rank as experience ; or whether I express myself thus : everything of which experience teaches me that it happens must have a cause.

It is however more convenient to choose the first formula. For as we can well have knowledge *a priori* and before any objects are given of those conditions under which alone an experience in respect of them is possible, but never knowledge of what laws they may be subject to in themselves without reference to possible experience, we shall not be able to study the nature of things *a priori* in any other way than by investigating the conditions and universal (although subjective) laws, under which alone such knowledge is possible as experience (merely according to form), and by determining accordingly the possibility of things as objects of experience. For if I were to choose the second way of expressing the problem, and to look for the conditions *a priori* under which nature is possible as *object* of experience, I could easily run into misunderstanding and imagine that I was talking of nature as a thing in itself, and I should be fruitlessly driven around in endless endeavours to seek laws for things of which nothing is given to me.

We shall here be concerned merely with experience and the universal conditions given *a priori* of its possibility, and shall determine nature from this as the whole object of all possible experience. I think it will be understood that I do not mean here the rules for *observing* a nature which is already given : these presuppose experience ; and hence not, how (by experience) we can learn laws from nature, for these would not then be laws *a priori* and would not yield pure natural science ; but how the conditions *a priori* of the possibility of experience are at the same time the sources from which all universal laws of nature must be derived.

§ 18

We must then first notice : that although all judgements of experience are empirical, i.e. have their ground in immediate sense perception, yet all empirical judgements are not conversely for that reason judgements of experience, but that in addition to the empirical and in general in addition to what is given to sensible intuition, special concepts which have their origin wholly *a priori* in pure understanding must still be added, under which every perception must first be subsumed before it can be changed into experience by their means.

Empirical judgements, so far as they have objective validity, are JUDGEMENTS OF EXPERIENCE ; those which are *only subjectively valid* I call mere JUDGEMENTS OF PERCEPTION. The latter do not need a pure concept of the understanding but only the logical connection of perception in a thinking subject. The former on the other hand always need, in addition to the representations of sensible intuition, special *concepts originally generated in the understanding*, and it is these that make the judgement of experience *objectively valid*.

All our judgements are at first mere judgements of perception, they are valid only for us, i.e. for our subject, and only afterwards do we give them a new reference, namely to an object, and want the judgement to be valid for us at all times and equally for everybody ; for if a judgement agrees with an object, all judgements about the same object must agree with one another, and thus the objective validity of the judgement of experience means nothing other than its necessary universal validity. And conversely if we find cause to hold a judgement to be necessarily universally valid (which never rests on perception but on the pure concept of the understanding under which the perception is subsumed) we must also hold it to be objective, i.e. that it expresses not merely a reference of the perception to a subject, but a quality of the object ; for there would be no reason why the judgements of others should necessarily agree with mine if it were not for the unity of the object to which all refer, with which they agree and hence must also all agree with one another.

§ 19

Objective validity and necessary universal validity (for everyone) are therefore identical concepts, and although we do not know the object in itself, yet when we regard a judgement as universally valid and necessary we mean by this its objective validity. We know the object through this judgement (even if otherwise, as to what it may be like in itself, it remains unknown), through the universally valid and necessary connection of the given perceptions. This being the case for all objects of the senses, judgements of experience will take their objective validity not from immediate knowledge of the object (for this is impossible), but merely from the condition of the universal validity of empirical judgements, which, as has been said, never rests on empirical conditions or indeed on sensible conditions at all, but on a pure concept of the understanding. The object in itself always remains unknown ; but when the connection of representations which are given to our sensibility by it is determined as universally valid by the concept of the understanding, the object is determined by this relation and the judgement is objective.

We proceed to illustrate this. That the room is warm, sugar is sweet, wormwood is nasty*, are merely subjectively

* I readily admit that these examples do not represent such judgements of perception as ever could become judgements of experience, even if a concept of the understanding were added, because they refer

valid judgements. I do not demand that I shall find it
so at all times, or every other person the same as I. They
only express a reference of two sensations to the same
subject, namely myself, and this only in my present state
of perception, and hence are not intended to be valid of
the object ; such judgements I call judgements of perception. Matters are quite different with the judgement of
experience. What experience teaches me under certain
circumstances, experience must teach me and everybody
always, and its validity is not limited to a particular subject
or to its state at a particular time. Hence I pronounce
all such judgements as objectively valid ; as for example
when I say air is elastic, this judgement is at first only a
judgement of perception, I only refer two sensations in my
senses to one another. But if I would have it called a
judgement of experience, I demand that this connection
shall stand under a condition which makes it universally
valid. I require that I and everybody must always necessarily conjoin the same perceptions under the same
circumstances.

§ 20

We shall therefore have to analyse experience in general,
in order to see what is contained in this product of the
senses and the understanding and how the judgement of
experience itself is possible. It is grounded on the intuition
of which I am conscious, i.e. perception (*perceptio*), which
belongs merely to the senses. But in the second place
there also belongs to it judging (which pertains merely to
the understanding). This judging can be of two kinds :

merely to feeling, which everyone recognises as subjective and which
can never be attributed to the object, and thus they can never become
objective. For the present I only wished to give an example of a judgement that is merely subjectively valid and contains in itself no ground
for necessary universal validity and thereby for reference to the object.
An example of judgements of perception that become judgements of
experience by an added concept of the understanding follows in the
next footnote.

first, in that I merely compare perceptions and conjoin them in a consciousness of my state, or secondly, when I conjoin them in a consciousness in general. The former judgement is merely a judgement of perception and has thus far only subjective validity ; it is merely the connecting of perceptions in the state of my mind, without reference to the object. Hence for experience it is not enough, as is commonly imagined, to compare perceptions and to connect them in a consciousness by means of judging ; through this there arises no universal validity and necessity of the judgement, by virtue of which alone it can be objectively valid and be experience.

Hence it is quite another judgement that precedes the turning of perception into experience. The given intuition must be subsumed under a concept which determines the form of judgement in general in respect of the intuition, connects the empirical consciousness of the intuition in a consciousness in general, and thereby provides the empirical judgements with universal validity. Such a concept is a pure concept of the understanding *a priori*, which does nothing but merely determine for an intuition the way in general in which it can serve for judging. If such a concept is the concept of cause, it determines the intuition which is subsumed under it, e.g. that of the air, in respect of judging in general, namely that the concept of air in respect of expansion serves in the relation of antecedent to consequent in a hypothetical judgement. The concept of cause is thus a pure concept of the understanding, which is wholly different from all possible perception, and only serves to determine the representation which is contained under it in respect of judging in general, and so to make possible a universally valid judgement.

Before a judgement of perception can become a judgement of experience, it is first required : that the perception shall be subsumed under such a concept of the understanding ; e.g. air belongs under the concept of cause, which determines a judgement about it in respect of extension as hypothetical.* This extension is thereby represented not as merely belonging to my perception of air in my state or in several of my states or in the state of perception of others, but as belonging to my perception of air *necessarily*. The judgement air is elastic becomes universally valid, and only then a judgement of experience, through being preceded by certain judgements which subsume the intuition of air under the concept of cause and effect, thereby determining the perceptions not merely in respect of one another in my subject, but in respect of the form of judging in general (here the hypothetical form), and in this way make the empirical judgement universally valid.

If one analyses all one's synthetic judgements so far as they are objectively valid, one finds that they never consist in mere intuitions which, as is commonly supposed, are merely connected in a judgement through comparison, but that they would be impossible if in addition to the concepts abstracted from intuition a pure concept of the understanding had not been added, under which these concepts have been subsumed and only then connected in an objectively valid judgement. Even the judgements of pure mathematics in its simplest axioms are not excepted from this condition. The principle: the straight line is the shortest between two points, presupposes that the line has been subsumed under the concept of quantity, which is certainly no mere intuition but has its seat solely in the understanding and serves to determine the intuition (of the line) with a view to the judgements that may be made

* For an easier example, take the following. When the sun shines on the stone, it grows warm. This judgement is a mere judgement of perception and contains no necessity, no matter how often I and others may have perceived this ; the perceptions are only usually found conjoined in this way. But if I say : the sun *warms* the stone, the concept of the understanding of cause is added to the perception and connects the concept of warmth *necessarily* with the concept of sunshine. The synthetic judgement becomes necessarily universally valid, consequently objective and is converted from a perception into experience.

about it in respect of its quantity, namely judgements of plurality (as *iudicia plurativa* *), in that it is understood by them that in a given intuition there is contained a homogeneous plurality.

§ 21

In order to show the possibility of experience in so far as it rests on pure concepts of the understanding *a priori*, we must first represent what belongs to judgements in general, and the different moments of the understanding in them, in a complete table. For the pure concepts of the understanding will fall exactly parallel to them, being nothing more than concepts of intuitions in general which are determined in themselves as judgements, necessarily and with universal validity, in respect of one or other of these moments. Through this the principles *a priori* of the possibility of all experience, as objectively valid empirical knowledge, will also be exactly determined. For they are nothing other than propositions which subsume all perception under the said pure concepts of the understanding (in conformity with certain universal conditions of intuition)[1].

* I should prefer this name for the judgements which are called in logic *particularia*. For this term already contains the thought that they are not universal. But when I begin from unity (in singular judgements) and proceed to totality,[2] I cannot yet include any reference to totality ; I only think plurality without totality, not the exclusion of totality. This is necessary if the logical moments are to underlie the pure concepts of the understanding ; in logical usage things can stay as they are.

---

[1] The term " physiological " in the following table is used in the obsolete sense " relating to the material universe or to natural science, physical ; belonging to the Physiologers as students of nature " (*O.E.D.*). Cf. § 23, last sentence.

[2] The sense seems to require " plurality " for " totality " here. Comparable errors occur elsewhere in the text of the original editions.

LOGICAL TABLE

OF JUDGEMENTS

1.

As to QUANTITY
Universal
Particular
Singular

2.
As to QUALITY
Affirmative
Negative
Infinite

3.
As to RELATION
Categorical
Hypothetical
Disjunctive

4.
As to MODALITY
Problematic
Assertoric
Apodictic

TRANSCENDENTAL TABLE

OF CONCEPTS OF THE UNDERSTANDING

1.

As to QUANTITY
Unity (measure)
Plurality (quantity)
Totality (the whole)

2.
Of QUALITY
Reality
Negation
Limitation

3.
Of RELATION [1]
Substance
Cause
Community

4.
Of MODALITY
Possibility
Existence
Necessity

PURE PHYSIOLOGICAL TABLE

OF UNIVERSAL PRINCIPLES OF NATURAL SCIENCE

1.

AXIOMS
of intuition

2.
ANTICIPATIONS
of perception

3.
ANALOGIES
of experience

4.
POSTULATES
of empirical thought
in general

---

[1] In the *Critique of Pure Reason* the categories of RELATION are given as at foot of next page.

§ 21 [1]

To reduce all that has been said so far to an epitome it is first necessary to remind the reader : that here we are not talking about the origin of experience but about what lies in it. The former belongs to empirical psychology and even there could never be properly developed without the latter, which belongs to the critique of knowledge and in particular of the understanding.

Experience consists of intuitions which belong to sensibility, and of judgements which are solely the business of the understanding. But those judgements which the understanding makes solely out of sensible intuitions are not by a long way judgements of experience. For in the one case the judgements would only connect the perceptions as they are given in sensible intuition, but in the latter case the judgements are to say what experience in general contains, and not what the mere perception, the validity of which is merely subjective, contains. In the judgement of experience therefore, in addition to the sensible intuition and its logical connection in a judgement (after the connection has been made general by comparison), something must be added which determines the judgement as necessary and thereby as universally valid. This can be nothing other than that concept which represents the intuition as determined in itself in respect of one form of judgement rather than another, i.e. a concept of that synthetic unity of intuitions which can only be represented by a given logical function of judgements.

§ 22

The sum of this is as follows. The business of the senses

[1] The original editions have § 21, as here ; the previous paragraph is also numbered § 21. Some modern editions number this § 22, and renumber the rest accordingly ; others number this § 21a.

of Inherence and Subsistence (*substantia et accidens*)
of Causality and Dependence (cause and effect)
of Community (reciprocity between the active and the passive)

is to intuit; that of the understanding, to think. Now thinking is unifying representations in a consciousness. This unification arises either merely relatively to the subject and is contingent and subjective, or it happens absolutely and is necessary or objective. Unification of representations in a consciousness is judgement. Therefore thinking is the same as judging, or referring representations to judgements in general. Hence judgements are either merely subjective, when representations are referred to a consciousness in one subject alone and are unified in it, or they are objective, when they are unified in a consciousness in general, i.e. necessarily unified in it. The logical moments of all judgements are so many possible ways of unifying representations in a consciousness. But if these serve as concepts, they are concepts of the *necessary* unification of representations in a consciousness and are principles of objectively valid judgements. This unification in a consciousness is either analytic through identity, or synthetic through the combination and addition of different representations with one another. Experience consists in the synthetic connection of appearances (perceptions) in a consciousness, so far as this connection is necessary. Hence pure concepts of the understanding are those under which all perceptions must first be subsumed, before they can be used for judgements of experience, in which the synthetic unity of perceptions is represented as necessary and universally valid.*

* But how does this proposition: that judgements of experience should contain necessity in the synthesis of perceptions, fit in with my proposition repeatedly inculcated above: that experience, as knowledge *a posteriori*, can only give contingent judgements? When I say experience teaches me something, I always mean only the perception that lies in it, e.g. that heat always follows illumination of the stone by the sun, and thus the proposition of experience is so far always contingent. That this heating necessarily follows from the illumination by the sun is indeed contained in the judgement of experience (by virtue of the concept of cause), but I do not learn this through experience; on the contrary, experience is only generated when the concept of the understanding (of cause) has been added to the perception. How the per-

§ 23

Judgements, in so far as they are considered merely as the condition of the unification of given representations in a consciousness, are rules. These rules, in so far as they represent the unification as necessary, are rules *a priori*, and in so far as there are none above them from which they can be deduced, they are principles. Now in respect of the possibility of all experience, considering in it merely the form of thought, there are no conditions of judgements of experience above those which bring appearances, according to the different form of their intuition, under pure concepts of the understanding which make the empirical judgement objectively valid. Hence these pure concepts of the understanding are the principles *a priori* of possible experience.

Now the principles of possible experience are at the same time universal laws of nature, which can be known *a priori*. And thus the problem which lies in the second question now before us : *How is pure natural science possible?* is solved. For the systematisation that is required for the form of a science is here to be found in perfection, because above the said formal conditions of all judgements in general and of all rules in general, which logic offers, no others are possible. These constitute a logical system, the concepts grounded therein, which contain the conditions *a priori* for all synthetic and necessary judgements, constitute for that reason a transcendental system, and finally the principles by means of which all appearances are subsumed under these concepts constitute a physiological system, i.e. a system of nature ; which system precedes all empirical knowledge of nature, first makes it possible, and

ception comes by this addition may be seen by referring to the Critique in the section on the transcendental judgement, p. 137 et seq.[1]

---

[1] i.e. *Critique of Pure Reason*, A137/B176, Transcendental Doctrine of Judgement, Chapter I, The Schematism of the Pure Concepts of the Understanding.

hence can properly be called universal and pure natural science.

§ 24

The first * of the above physiological principles [1] subsumes all appearances, as intuitions in space and time, under the concept of *quantity*, and is thus a principle of the application of mathematics to experience. The second [2] subsumes what is properly empirical, namely sensation, which denotes what is real in intuitions, not directly under the concept of *quantity*, because sensation is not intuition and so does not *contain* space and time, even though it posits the object corresponding to itself in both; but between reality (sensible representation) and zero, i.e. the complete absence of intuition in time, there is still a difference which has a quantity; for between any given degree of light and darkness, between any degree of heat and complete cold, any degree of weight and absolute lightness, any degree of occupation of space and wholly empty space, still smaller degrees can be thought, and even between consciousness and complete unconsciousness (psychological obscurity) still smaller degrees of consciousness find a place. Hence no perception is possible which would show absolute deficiency, e.g. no psychological obscurity which could not be regarded as a consciousness only surpassed by another stronger consciousness,[3] and

---

* The reader will hardly be able to understand this and the two following paragraphs properly [4] without referring to what the Critique says about principles;[5] but they may be of use in making it easier to survey their general features and drawing attention to the main moments.

[1] The axioms of intuition.

[2] The anticipations of perception.

[3] i.e. than which there are stronger but no weaker degrees of consciousness.

[4] These three paragraphs are written in a highly condensed and obscure language.

[5] The section of the *Critique of Pure Reason* called "Analytic of Principles".

likewise in all cases of sensation. For this reason the understanding can anticipate sensations, which properly constitute the quality of empirical representations (appearances), by means of the principle that all sensations without exception have degrees, and thus what is real in all appearance has degrees. This is the second application of mathematics (*mathesis intensorum*) to natural science.

§ 25

In respect of the relation of appearances, solely with regard to their existence, the determination of this relation is not mathematical but dynamic, and can never be objectively valid and fit for experience if it does not stand under principles *a priori* [1] which first make possible knowledge by experience in respect of it. Hence appearances must be subsumed under the concept of substance, which, as a concept of the thing itself, lies at the ground of all determination of existence ; or secondly, in the case of a succession in time among the appearances i.e. an event, under the concept of an effect in reference to a cause ; or in the case of contemporaneity which is to be known objectively i.e. through a judgement of experience, under the concept of community (reciprocity). Thus principles *a priori* lie at the ground of objectively valid though empirical judgements ; that is to say, they lie at the ground of the possibility of experience in so far as it is to connect objects in nature according to existence. These principles are properly the laws of nature and can be called dynamic.

Finally [2] there also belongs to judgements of experience knowledge of the agreement and connection, not only of appearances among themselves in experience, but rather their relation [3] to experience in general. This knowledge contains either their agreement with the formal conditions

[1] The analogies of experience.

[2] The postulates of empirical thought in general.

[3] An emendation which would be translated " in relation " has been proposed.

which the understanding knows, or their connection with
the material of the senses and of perception, or combines
both in one concept, and consequently contains possibility,
reality and necessity according to universal laws of nature.
This would constitute the physiological doctrine of method
(distinction between truth and hypotheses, and the bounds
of the reliability of the latter).

§ 26

It is true that the third table, of principles drawn according to the critical method *from the nature of the understanding
itself*, displays a perfection which raises it far above every
other table *of the things themselves* that has ever been
attempted, although vainly, in the dogmatic way, or may
be attempted in the future.   For in my table all synthetic
principles *a priori* have been worked out completely and
according to a principle, namely the faculty of judging in
general which constitutes the essence of experience from
the viewpoint of the understanding.   One can thus be certain that there are no more such principles (a satisfaction
that the dogmatic method can never provide).   Yet all this
is by a long way not its greatest merit.

We must pay attention to the ground of proof which
reveals the possibility of this knowledge *a priori* and at the
same time limits all such principles to a condition which
must never be overlooked if they are not to be misunderstood and extended in use further than the original sense
which the understanding places in them will allow :
namely that they only contain the conditions of possible
experience in general so far as it is subjected to laws *a
priori*.   Thus I do not say : that things *in themselves* contain
a quantity, their reality a degree, their existence connection
of accidents in a substance, etc ; for nobody can prove this
because, when on the one hand all reference to sensible
intuition and on the other all connection of intuition in a
possible experience are lacking, such a synthetic connection
out of mere concepts is absolutely impossible.   The essential

limitation of the concepts in these principles is therefore : that all things stand necessarily *a priori* under the said conditions only *as objects of experience.*

From this it follows secondly that there is a specifically peculiar mode of proof of these principles : that they are also not referred directly to appearances and their relation, but to the possibility of experience, of which appearances only constitute the matter but not the form, i.e. they are referred to objectively and universally valid synthetic propositions, which is the distinction of judgements of experience from mere judgements of perception. This happens as follows : [1] appearances, as mere intuitions *which occupy a part of space and time*, stand under the concept of quantity which unites the manifold of intuitions synthetically and *a priori* according to rules ; besides intuition, perception also contains sensation between which and zero, i.e. its complete disappearance, a transition by diminution always finds a place, and hence what is real in appearances must have degree, namely through sensation itself *occupying no part of space and time* * but the transition to sensation from empty time or space being only possible in time ; and although sensation, as the quality of empirical intuition in respect of its specific difference from other sensations, can never be known *a priori*, in a possible experience in general it can still be distinguished intensively as quantity

---

* Heat, light, etc. are just as large (in degree) in a small space as in a large one ; equally inner representations, pain, consciousness in general are not smaller in degree, whether they last for a short or a long time. Hence the quantity here is as great in a point and a moment as in any space or time however large. Degrees are thus quantities not in intuition but according to mere sensation or the quantity of the ground of an intuition, and can only be estimated as quantities through the relation of 1 to 0, i.e. through any of them being able to decrease by infinite intermediate degrees to disappearance, or to increase from zero by infinite moments of growth to a determinate sensation, in a certain time. (*Quantitas qualitatis est gradus.*)[2]

---

[1] The mode of proof of the mathematical principles (the axioms of intuition and the anticipations of perception).

[2] " The quantity of quality is degree."

of perception from any other of the same kind.   From this
the application of mathematics to nature, in respect of the
sensible intuition through which it is given to us, is first
made possible and determined.

But the reader [1] must pay greatest attention to the mode
of proof of the principles which occur under the name of
the Analogies of Experience.   Because these do not concern the generation of intuitions, like the principles of the
application of mathematics to natural science in general,
but the connection of their existence in an experience ;
and because this can be nothing other than the determination of existence in time according to necessary laws, under
which alone it is objectively valid and thus is experience :
for these reasons the proof does not bear on the synthetic
unity in the connection *of things* in themselves but only of
perceptions, and of these not in respect of their content but
of the time-determination and relation of existence in time,
according to universal laws.   These universal laws thus
contain the necessity of the determination of existence in
time in general (consequently according to a rule of the
understanding *a priori*), if the empirical determination in
relative time is to be objectively valid, and thus to be
experience.   For the reader who retains his long habit of
taking experience for a merely empirical synthesis of
perceptions and hence never thinks of the fact that it goes
much further than perceptions reach, in that it gives
universal validity to empirical judgements and needs for
this a pure unity of the understanding preceding it *a priori*,
I can do no more here, these being prolegomena, than to
recommend him to heed well this difference between
experience and a mere aggregate of perceptions, and to
judge the mode of proof from this point of view.

§ 27

This is now the place to dispose of the HUMEAN doubt
once and for all.   He asserted, rightly, that we can in no

[1] The reader of the *Critique of Pure Reason.*

way have insight by reason into the possibility of causality, i.e. of the reference of the existence of a thing to the existence of something else which is posited necessarily by the first. I add that we have equally little insight into the concept of subsistence, i.e. of the necessity that there must lie at the ground of the existence of things a subject which cannot itself be a predicate of anything else, indeed that we can make for ourselves no concept of the possibility of such a thing (although we can point to examples of its use in experience); similarly that this same inconceivability touches the community of things, in that we can have no insight into how a consequence can be drawn from the state of one thing to the state of quite other things outside it, and reciprocally, and how substances, each one of which has its own separate existence, can be dependent on one another necessarily. None the less I am far from holding that these concepts are merely taken from experience and that the necessity which is represented in them is fictitious and mere illusion imposed on us by long habit; on the contrary I have shown adequately that these concepts and the principles drawn from them stand *a priori* before all experience and have their undoubted objective rightness, though admittedly only in respect of experience.

§ 28

Although I cannot in the least conceive of any such connection of things in themselves, how they can exist as substances or have effects as causes or be in community with others (as parts of a real whole), and although I can still less think such properties in appearances as appearances (because these concepts contain nothing that lies in appearances; what they contain is something that the understanding alone must think), yet equally we can conceive of such a connection of representations in our understanding, namely in judgements in general. This is the concept that representations belong in one kind of judgement as subject in reference to predicates, in another kind as ground in reference to consequence, and in a third kind as parts which together make up a whole of possible knowledge. We know further *a priori* : that unless we regard the representation of an object as determined in respect of one or other of these moments, we could have no knowledge which would be valid of the object ; and if we occupied ourselves with the object in itself, not a single mark would be possible by which I could recognise that it was determined in respect of one or other of the said moments, i.e. belonged under the concept of substance or of cause or (in relation to other substances) under the concept of community ; for I cannot conceive of the possibility of such a connection of existence. But the question is not how things in themselves are determined but how knowledge of things by experience is determined in respect of the said moments of judgements in general, i.e. how things, as objects of experience, can be and are to be subsumed under these concepts of the understanding. And then it is clear that I have perfect insight not only into the possibility but also into the necessity of subsuming all appearances under these concepts, i.e. into using them as principles of the possibility of experience.

§ 29

To put to a test HUME's problematic concept (which was his *crux metaphysicorum*), namely the concept of cause : first, the form of a conditional judgement in general, namely using a given piece of knowledge as ground and another as consequence, is given to me *a priori* by means of logic. But it is possible that in perception a rule of relation will be encountered, which will say : that a certain appearance is followed constantly by another (though not conversely) ; and this will be a case for me to use the hypothetical judgement, and for example to say, if the sun shines long enough on a body, it grows warm. Admittedly there is as yet no necessity in the connection, and no concept of cause. But I continue and say : if the above proposition which is merely a subjective connection of perceptions is to be a proposition of experience, it must be regarded as necessary and universally valid. Such a proposition would be : the sun through its light is the cause of heat. The above empirical rule is now regarded as a law, and as one not valid merely of appearances, but valid of them on behalf of a possible experience, which needs comprehensively and therefore necessarily valid rules. Thus I do very well have insight into the concept of cause, as a concept necessarily belonging to the mere form of experience, and into its possibility as synthetic unification of perceptions in a consciousness in general ; but I have no insight at all into the possibility of a thing in general as a cause, because the concept of cause indicates a condition not attached in any way whatever to things, but only to experience, namely, that experience can only be an objectively valid knowledge of appearances and of their sequence in time when the antecedent appearances can be joined with the subsequent appearances according to the rule of hypothetical judgements.

§ 30

Hence the pure concepts of the understanding also have no meaning whatever if they try to leave objects of experience and to be referred to things in themselves (noumena). They serve as it were only to spell out appearances, so that they can be read as experience ; the principles which arise from their reference to the world of the senses only serve our understanding for use in experience ; beyond it they are arbitrary connections without objective reality, the possibility of which cannot be known *a priori*, nor their reference to objects confirmed by any example, or even made understandable, because all examples can only be taken from some possible experience, and the objects of those concepts can also be found nowhere else than in a possible experience.

This complete solution to the HUMEAN problem, although

it turns out contrary to the expectation of its originator, thus rescues their *a priori* origin for the pure concepts of the understanding, and their validity for the universal laws of nature, as laws of the understanding ; but in such a way that it limits their use to experience only, because their possibility has its ground merely in the reference of the understanding to experience ; not in such a way that they are deduced from experience but that experience is deduced from them, a completely reversed kind of connection which never occurred to HUME.

From this there flows the following result of all the foregoing researches : " All synthetic principles *a priori* are nothing more than principles of possible experience " and can never be referred to things in themselves, but only to appearances as objects of experience. Hence pure mathematics as well as pure natural science can never bear on anything more than mere appearances, and can only represent either that which makes experience in general possible, or that which, as deduced from these principles, must always be capable of being represented in some possible experience.

§ 31

And thus we now at last have something determinate and something to hold on to in all metaphysical undertakings, which hitherto, bold enough but always blind, have taken on everything without distinction. It has never occurred to dogmatic thinkers that the target of their exertions should be set up so close, nor even to those thinkers proud of their supposed common sense who, with concepts and principles of pure reason which were indeed legitimate and natural, but destined merely for use in experience, went after insights for which they knew and could know no determinate bounds, because they had never reflected nor been able to reflect on the nature and even the possibility of such a pure understanding.

Many a naturalist of pure reason (by which I mean the

man who trusts himself to decide in matters of metaphysics without any science) may well pretend that long since, through the second sight of his common sense, he has not merely guessed but known and had insight into what is here propounded with so much preparation, or, if he prefers, with prolix pedantic pomp, namely " that with all our reason we can never get outside the field of experiences ". But as he has to admit, when his principles of reason are gradually questioned out of him, that many of them have not been drawn from experience, and therefore are independent of it and valid *a priori*, how and on what grounds will he then keep the dogmatist (and himself) within limits, who is using these concepts and principles outside all possible experience, precisely because they are known independently of experience ? And even he, this adept of common sense, is not so certain, in spite of all his pretension to cheaply acquired wisdom, that he will not go insensibly outside the objects of experience into the field of chimeras. Ordinarily he is indeed deeply enough involved in them though he gives colour to his groundless claims by his popular language, in which he announces everything merely as probability, rational conjecture or analogy.

§ 32

Since the earliest times of philosophy enquirers into pure reason have thought that, besides the beings of the senses or appearances (*phaenomena*) which constitute the world of the senses, there were special beings of the understanding (*noumena*), which were supposed to constitute a world of the understanding. As they took appearance and illusion to be the same (which can well be excused in an as yet uncouth age), they allowed reality only to the beings of the understanding.

In fact, if we regard the objects of the senses, as is proper, as mere appearances, we admit at the same time by so doing that they have a thing in itself as their ground, although we do not know what it is like in itself, but only know its appearance, i.e. the way in which our senses are affected by this unknown something.   Thus understanding, precisely by accepting appearances, also admits the existence of things in themselves, and thus far we can say that the representation of such beings which lie at the ground of appearances, and are mere beings of the understanding, is not merely admissible but is unavoidable.

Our critical deduction in no way excludes such things (*noumena*), but rather limits the principles of aesthetic [1] in such a way that they are not to extend to all things, by which everything would be transformed into mere appearance, but are to be valid only of objects of a possible experience.   Thus beings of the understanding are admitted, but under inculcation of this rule which suffers no exception : that we know and can know nothing determinate whatever about these pure beings of the understanding, because both our pure concepts of the understanding and our pure intuitions bear on nothing but objects of possible experience, which are mere beings of the senses, and as soon as we depart from these not the slightest meaning is left to those concepts.

§ 33

There is in fact something captious about our pure concepts of the understanding, in respect of the temptation to a transcendent use of them ; for that is what I call the use that goes beyond all possible experience.   Not only that our concepts of substance, force, action, reality etc., are quite independent of experience and contain no appearance of the senses, consequently in fact seem to refer to things in themselves (*noumena*) ; but also, to strengthen this supposition still further, they contain in themselves a necessity of determination which experience

---

[1] " Aesthetic " in the sense of the *Critique of Pure Reason*, i.e. the principles of sensibility (space and time).   An emendation to " analytic " has been proposed.

never attains. The concept of cause contains a rule according to which one state follows from another necessarily ; but experience can only show us that one state of things often or, at most, commonly follows another, and can procure neither strict universality nor necessity, etc.

Hence concepts of the understanding seem to have much more meaning and content than if their whole destiny were exhausted in their use merely in experience, and so the understanding insensibly builds on to the house of experience a much more extensive wing which it fills up with nothing but beings of thought, without ever noticing that with its otherwise correct concepts it has transgressed the boundaries of their use.

§ 34

Two important, indeed quite indispensable, although extremely dry enquiries were therefore needed, and were undertaken in the Critique pages 137&c and 235&c.[1] In the first it was shown that the senses only provide the schema for the use of the pure concepts of the understanding, not the pure concepts of the understanding *in concreto*, and that the object conforming to the schema is encountered only in experience (this being the product of the understanding out of the materials of sensibility). In the second enquiry (Critique, p. 235) the following is shown. Notwithstanding the independence of our pure concepts of the understanding and principles from experience, notwithstanding indeed the apparently greater extent of their use, nothing can be thought through them outside the field of experience, because they can do nothing but merely determine the logical form of the judgement in respect of given intuitions ; and as there is no intuition whatever outside the field of sensibility, these pure concepts

[1] i.e. *Critique of Pure Reason*, A137/B176, Of the Schematism of the Pure Concepts of the Understanding, and A235/B294, The Ground of the Distinction of all Objects in General into Phaenomena and Noumena.

have no meaning whatever, for there is no means of exhibiting them *in concreto*. Consequently all such *Noumena*, together with the totality of them, an intelligible * world, are nothing but representations of a problem the object of which in itself is well possible ; but its solution, because of the nature of our understanding, is wholly impossible, in that our understanding is not a faculty of intuition but merely a faculty of the connection of given intuitions in an experience. Hence experience must contain all the objects for our concepts, but beyond it all concepts will be without meaning as no intuition can be subsumed under them.

§ 35

The imagination can perhaps be forgiven if it is sometimes extravagant, i.e. does not carefully keep within the limits of experience, for it is at least enlivened and strengthened by such free flight, and it will always be easier to moderate its boldness than to revive its faintness. But for the understanding, which ought to *think*, to *extravagate* instead, can never be forgiven ; for all help in setting bounds, where needed, to the extravagance of the imagination depends on it alone.

The understanding begins its extravagance very innocently and modestly. It first distinguishes the elementary knowledge which is present in it prior to all experience, but yet must always have its application in experience. Gradually it leaves these limits out, and what is indeed to prevent it, as the understanding has taken its principles quite freely from within itself? And now it first goes for

* Not (as the usual expression is) *intellectual* world. For *knowledge* is *intellectual* through the *understanding*, and such knowledge also refers to the world of our senses ; but *objects* are called *intelligible* in so far as they can be represented *merely by the understanding* and none of our sensible intuitions can refer to them. But as every object must have some possible intuition corresponding to it, one would have to think an understanding which intuited things immediately ; but of such an understanding we do not have the least concept, nor of *beings of the understanding* on which it would bear.

newly thought out forces in nature, soon after for beings outside nature, in a word for a world for the furnishing of which we cannot lack for material, because it is abundantly provided by fruitful fiction, not, it is true, confirmed by experience, but also never refuted. That is also the reason why young thinkers are so much in love with metaphysics in the genuine dogmatic manner, and often sacrifice to it their time and their otherwise useful talent.

But there is no help in trying to moderate those fruitless attempts of pure reason by all kinds of reminders about the difficulty of solving questions hidden so deeply, by complaints about the limits of our reason, and by the reducing of assertions to mere conjectures. For if their *impossibility* has not been clearly exhibited and the *self-knowledge* of reason does not become true science, in which the field of its correct use is distinguished, so to speak with geometrical certainty, from the field of its empty and fruitless use, those vain endeavours will never be completely abandoned.

How is Nature itself possible ?

§ 36

This question, which is the highest point that transcendental philosophy can ever touch and is also its boundary and completion, up to which it must be taken, properly contains two questions.

First : How is nature possible in general in the *material* sense, namely according to intuition, as the totality of appearances ; how are space, time and that which fills both, the object of sensation, possible in general ? The answer is : by means of the quality of our sensibility, according to which it is affected, in its peculiar way, by objects which are in themselves unknown and quite different from those appearances. This answer has been given in the book itself in the Transcendental Aesthetic, and here in the Prolegomena by the solution of the first main question.

Secondly : How is nature in the *formal* sense possible, as the totality of rules under which all appearances must stand if they are to be thought as connected in an experience ? The answer cannot be other than this : nature is possible only by means of the quality of our understanding, according to which all those representations of sensibility are necessarily referred to a consciousness, and through which alone the peculiar kind of our thinking, namely through rules, is possible ; and by means of this, experience is possible, which is wholly to be distinguished from insight into objects in themselves. This answer has been given in the book itself in the Transcendental Logic, and here in the Prolegomena in the course of the solution of the second main question.

But how this peculiar property of our sensibility itself is possible, and how that of our understanding and of the necessary apperception lying at the ground of the understanding and of all thought are possible, cannot be further analysed and answered, because we always have to use them for all answering and for all our thinking of objects.

There are many laws of nature that we can only know by means of experience, but conformity to law in the connection of appearances, i.e. nature in general, we can get to know through no experience, because experience itself needs such laws, which lie *a priori* at the ground of its possibility.

The possibility of experience in general is thus at the same time the universal law of nature, and the principles of the former are themselves the laws of the latter. For we know nature in no other way than as the totality of appearances, i.e. of representations in us, and hence there is nothing from which we can derive the law of their connection but the principles of their connection in us, i.e. from the conditions of necessary unification in a consciousness, which constitutes the possibility of experience.

The main proposition, expounded throughout this whole section, that universal laws of nature can be known *a priori*, leads of itself to the proposition that the highest legislation of nature must lie in ourselves, i.e. in our understanding, and that we must not seek the universal laws of nature from nature by means of experience, but conversely, we must seek nature, as to its universal conformity to law, merely from the conditions of the possibility of experience which lie in our sensibility and in the understanding. For how would it otherwise be possible to know these laws *a priori*, as they are not rules of analytical knowledge, but genuine synthetic extensions of it? Such agreement, which is a necessary agreement, between the principles of possible experience and the laws of the possibility of nature, can only take place for two reasons : either these laws are borrowed from nature by means of experience, or conversely nature is deduced from the laws of the possibility of experience in general, and is entirely the same as the mere universal conformity to law of the latter. The former is self-contradictory, for the universal laws of nature can and must be known *a priori* (i.e. independently of all experience) and be placed at the ground of all empirical use of the understanding ; thus only the second is left.*

But we must distinguish empirical laws of nature, which always presuppose particular perceptions, from the pure or

---

* CRUSIUS [1] alone knew of a middle way : namely that a spirit which cannot err nor deceive would have originally implanted these laws of nature in us. But as false principles often intrude themselves, of which this man's System itself offers not a few examples, it looks very dangerous to use such a principle in the absence of sure criteria for distinguishing the genuine origin from the spurious, for we can never know for sure what may have been instilled in us by the Spirit of Truth and what by the Father of Lies.

---

[1] Christian August Crusius (1715–75), published a number of philosophical works between 1740 and 1750, including an Ethics (1744), a Metaphysics (1745), a Logic (1747) and a Physics (1749). The most influential opponent of the Leibniz-Wolffian philosophy, he criticised the doctrine of optimism and the principle of sufficient reason. The world contains free beings (spirits) and absolute necessity is not universal. He used the veracity of God as one of the guarantees of the existence of the outside world and the truth of principles.

universal laws of nature, which without having particular perceptions as their ground merely contain the conditions of their necessary unification in an experience.   In respect of the latter, nature and *possible* experience are exactly the same, and as, in the latter, conformity to law rests on the necessary connection of appearances in an experience (without which we can know no object whatever in the world of the senses) and on the original laws of the understanding, it sounds strange at first, but is not less certain for that, when I say in respect of the latter : *the understanding does not draw its laws (a priori) from nature, but prescribes them to nature.*

§ 37

We shall illustrate this apparently daring proposition by an example, which is intended to show : that laws which we discover in objects of sensible intuition, especially when they are recognised as necessary, are already held by us to be laws that the understanding has placed in them, although they are otherwise similar in all respects to the laws of nature which we ascribe to experience.

§ 38

If we consider the properties of the circle, through which this figure at once combines into a universal rule so many arbitrary determinations of the space in it, we cannot avoid giving to this geometrical thing a nature.   Thus two lines, which cut each other and the circle, in whatever haphazard way they may be drawn, always divide each other regularly, so that the rectangle erected on the segments of either line is equal to that on the segments of the other.   Now I ask : " does this law lie in the circle or does it lie in the understanding ? " i.e. does this figure, independently of the understanding, contain the ground of this law in itself, or does the understanding put into it the law of the chords cutting each other in geometrical proportion when it constructs the figure itself according to its concepts (namely of the equality of the radii) ?   One soon perceives, if one pursues the proofs of this law, that it can be deduced solely from the condition which the understanding placed at the ground of the construction of this figure, namely the equality of the radii. If we enlarge this concept, to pursue further the unity of manifold properties of geometrical figures under common laws, and consider the circle as a conic section, which thus stands with other conic sections under the same fundamental conditions of construction, we find that all chords which intersect inside the latter, the ellipse, the parabola and hyperbola, always do so in such a way that the rectangles erected on their segments, though not equal, always stand in the same relations to each other. If we go still further, to the fundamental doctrines of physical astronomy, we find a physical law of reciprocal attraction extending over the whole material nature, the rule of which is that it decreases inversely with the square of the distances of each attracting point, just as the spherical surfaces in which this force diffuses itself increase, which seems to lie necessarily in the nature of things themselves and hence is usually propounded as capable of being known *a priori*. Simple as are the sources of this law, in that they rest merely on the relation of spherical surfaces of different radii, its consequence is so excellent in respect of the variety and regularity of its agreement, that it follows not only that all possible orbits of heavenly bodies are conic sections, but that they have such a relation to each other that no other law of attraction than that of the inverse square of the distances can be conceived as suitable for a cosmic system.

Here then is nature resting on laws which the understanding knows *a priori* and mainly from universal principles of the determination of space. Now I ask : do these laws of nature lie in space, and does the understanding learn them by merely trying to investigate the wealth of meaning that lies in space, or do they lie in the understanding and in the way in which the understanding determines space according to the conditions of synthetic unity to which all its concepts point? Space is something so homogeneous and in respect of all particular properties so indeterminate that there is certainly no hoard of natural laws to be found in it. On the other hand, that which determines space into the figure of the circle, the cone and the sphere, is the understanding, in that it contains the ground of the unity of the construction of these figures. The mere universal form of intuition that is called space is indeed the substratum of all intuitions which can be designated to particular objects, and admittedly there lies in space the condition of the possibility and variety of intuitions. But the unity of objects is determined solely by the understanding, and according to conditions which lie in the nature of the understanding. Thus in that it subsumes all appearances under its own laws and only by so doing brings into being experience (as to its form) *a priori*, the understanding is the origin of the universal order of nature, by virtue of which everything that is only to be known through experience is necessarily submitted to its laws. For we are concerned not with the nature *of things in themselves*, which is independent of the conditions both of our sensibility and of the understanding, but with nature as an object of possible experience, and there the understanding brings it about, at the same time as it makes nature possible, that the world of the senses is either not an object of experience at all, or is nature.

§ 39

Appendix to Pure Natural Science
Of the System of the Categories

Nothing can be more desirable to a philosopher than to be able to deduce the manifold of concepts or principles, which had previously exhibited themselves to him sporadically through the use that he had made of them *in concreto*, from one principle *a priori*, and in this way to unite everything in one kind of knowledge. Previously he merely believed that when he had made certain abstractions and

what was left over seemed by mutual comparison to constitute a particular kind of knowledge, he had assembled it
completely ; but it was only an *aggregate*. Now he knows
that only exactly so much, no more, no less, can constitute
this kind of knowledge, and has had insight into the necessity of his division ; which is to understand it. And not
until now does he have a *System*.

To seek out from ordinary knowledge the concepts which
are not grounded on any particular experience and none
the less occur in all knowledge by experience, of which they
constitute as it were the mere form of connection, presupposes no greater reflection or more insight than to seek out
from a language rules of the real use of words in general
and thus to collect the elements for a grammar (in fact
both enquiries are very closely related to one another),
without being able to state the ground, why any language
has exactly this and no other formal nature, and still less
that exactly so many, not more nor less, of such formal
determinations of language can ever be encountered.

ARISTOTLE collected ten such pure elementary concepts
under the name of categories.* To these, which were also
called predicaments, he later found himself compelled to
add five postpredicaments †, which are partly included
already in the former (*prius, simul, motus*) ; but this rhapsody
was valid and merited applause rather as a hint for future
enquirers than as a regularly worked out idea. Hence
with the greater enlightenment of philosophy it has been
rejected as quite useless.

On enquiring into the pure elements of human knowledge (those containing nothing empirical) I succeeded only
after long reflection in reliably distinguishing and separat-
ing the pure elementary concepts of sensibility (space and
time) from those of the understanding. In this way the
7th, 8th and 9th categories were excluded from the above

---

* 1. Substantia. 2. Qualitas. 3. Quantitas. 4. Relatio. 5. Actio.
6. Passio. 7. Quando. 8. Ubi. 9. Situs. 10. Habitus.
  † Oppositum, Prius, Simul, Motus, Habere.

list. The rest could be of no use to me, because no principle was present according to which the understanding could be fully mapped out and all its functions, from which its pure concepts arise, precisely determined in their total number.

In order to find such a principle I looked round for an act of the understanding which contains all the rest and is only differentiated by different modifications or moments, to bring the manifold of representation under the unity of thought in general. I found that this act of the understanding consists in judging. Here the work of the logicians lay before me, finished though not completely free of defects, and put me in the position to draw up a complete table of pure functions of the understanding, which were yet undetermined in respect of any object. Finally, I referred these functions of judging to objects in general, or rather to the condition of determining judgements as objectively valid, and there arose pure concepts of the understanding, of which I knew beyond doubt that exactly these, and only so many of them, not more or less, could constitute our whole knowledge of things out of mere understanding. I called them, as was proper, by their old name of *Categories*; while I reserved to myself to add all concepts derivable from these, either by connecting the categories with each other, or with the pure form of appearance (space and time), or with their matter in so far as it is not empirically determined (object of sensation in general); such a comprehensive addition under the name of *Predicables* was to be made as soon as a system of transcendental philosophy, for the purposes of which I was now only concerned with the critique of reason itself, should come into being.

Now the essential thing in this system of categories, by which it is distinguished from that ancient rhapsody that proceeded without any principle, and by reason of which this system alone deserves to be reckoned as philosophy, consists in this : by means of it the true meaning of the pure concepts of the understanding and the condition of their use could be exactly determined. For it became apparent that in themselves they are nothing but logical functions, and as such constitute not the slightest concept of an object in itself, but require sensible intuition as their ground. Empirical judgements being otherwise undetermined and indifferent in respect of all functions of judging, the pure concepts of the understanding then serve only to determine empirical judgements in respect of functions of judging, to procure thereby universal validity for them, and by means of them to make possible *judgements of experience* in general.

Nothing of such an insight into the nature of the categories, which would at the same time limit their use merely to experience, occurred to their first originator, or to anyone after him ; but without this insight (which depends exactly on the deduction of them) they are wholly useless and a miserable list of names without explanation or rule for their use. If any such insight had ever come into the mind of the ancients, there can be no doubt that the whole study of pure knowledge by reason, which under the name of metaphysics has been for many centuries the ruin of many a good brain, would have come to us in quite a different shape, and would have enlightened the understanding of men, instead of exhausting it in obscure and vain subtleties, as really happened, and making it unusable for true science.

This system of categories makes all treatment of any object of pure reason systematic itself in its turn, and yields an undoubted instruction or clue as to how and through what points of enquiry any metaphysical consideration must be taken if it is to be complete ; for it exhausts all the moments of the understanding, under which every other concept must be brought. The table of principles arose in the same way. One can be certain of its completeness only through the system of categories, and even in the division of the concepts which are to go beyond the physiological use of the understanding (Critique, p. 344, also

p. 415 [1]), it is still the same clue which, because it must always be taken through the same fixed points determined *a priori* in the human understanding, always forms a closed circle, leaving no room for doubt that the object of a pure concept of the understanding or of reason, in so far as it is to be considered philosophically and according to principles *a priori*, can be completely known in such a way. In addition I could not forbear to make use of this clue in respect of one of the most abstract ontological divisions, namely the manifold distinction of the *concepts of something and nothing*, and accordingly to draw up a regular and necessary table * (Critique p. 292 [2]).

* All kinds of pretty observations can be made about the above table of categories, for instance : 1) that the third arises out of the combination of the first and second in one concept ; 2) that in the concepts of quantity and quality there is merely a progress from unity to totality, or from something to nothing (for this purpose the categories of quality must stand thus : Reality, Limitation, complete Negation) without *correlata* or *opposita*, whereas those of relation and modality include these latter. 3) that as in *Logic* categorical judgements are the ground of all others, so the category of substance is the ground of all concepts of real things. 4) that as the modality in a judgement is not a distinct predicate, so the modal concepts add no determination to things, etc. Such observations all have their great utility. Moreover, if one reckons up all the *predicables*, which one can take, fairly completely, from any good Ontology (e.g. BAUMGARTEN's) and arranges them in classes under the categories, not omitting to add as complete an analysis as possible of all these concepts, a merely analytical part of metaphysics will arise, which will contain no synthetic proposition and could precede the second part (the synthetic). Through its determinateness and completeness it would contain not utility alone but in addition, by virtue of the system in it, a certain beauty.

[1] i.e. *Critique of Pure Reason*, A344/B402, Of the Paralogisms of Pure Reason (table of the four elements of rational psychology, derived from the categories : the soul is substance, simple, unity, and in relation to possible objects in space), and A415/B442-3, The Antinomy of Pure Reason, System of the Cosmological Ideas (table of the four cosmological ideas, composition, division, origination, and dependence of existence, derived from the categories).

[2] i.e. *Critique of Pure Reason*, A292/B348 (table of the four divisions of the concept of nothing, derived from the categories : *ens rationis, nihil privativum, ens imaginarium, nihil negativum*).

This same system, like every true system grounded on a universal principle, shows its inestimable use in that it also ejects all alien concepts, which might otherwise slip in among the pure concepts of the understanding, and gives all knowledge its proper place. In ontology, those concepts which under the name of *concepts of reflection* I had also made into a table according to the clue of the categories, mingle among the pure concepts of the understanding without sufferance or legitimate claims, although the latter are concepts of connection and thereby of the object itself, whereas the former are only concepts of the mere comparison of concepts already given, and hence have quite a different nature and use ; my distinction, made in conformity with a law (Critique, p. 260 [1]), separates them out of this confusion. The utility of this separate table of categories will be still more clearly obvious when, as will shortly happen, we distinguish from the categories the table of transcendental concepts of reason, which are of quite a different nature and origin from the concepts of the understanding (hence the table must have a different form). This very necessary separation has never happened in any system of metaphysics, where ideas of reason intermingle without distinction with concepts of the understanding, as if they belonged like brothers to one family, which confusion, in the absence of a distinct system of categories, could never be avoided.

[1] i.e. *Critique of Pure Reason*, A260/B316, The Amphiboly of the Concepts of Reflection. (The concepts of reflection are identity and difference, agreement and opposition, inner and outer, matter and form.)

How is Metaphysics possible in general?

§ 40

A deduction such as we have now made both of pure mathematics and of pure natural science was not needed by either of them *for the sake of their own security* and certainty ; for the first is supported on its own evidence ; and the second springs from pure sources of reason, although it is supported on experience and thoroughgoing confirmation by it, which latter witness it cannot altogether refuse and dispense with because with all its certainty, it can never, as philosophy,[1] stand equal with mathematics. Both sciences therefore needed the said enquiry not for themselves but for another science, namely metaphysics.

Metaphysics has to do, not only with concepts of nature which always find their application in experience, but also with pure concepts of reason which are never given in any possible experience whatever, that is, with concepts whose objective reality (that they are not mere chimeras) and assertions whose truth or falsehood can never be confirmed or discovered by any experience.   This part of metaphysics is moreover the one which constitutes the essential end of metaphysics, towards which everything else is only a means, and thus this science needs such a deduction *for its own sake*. The third question now before us concerns as it were the kernel of metaphysics and what is peculiar to it, namely the occupation of reason merely with itself and the acquaintance with objects which, brooding over its own concepts, it supposes to arise immediately out of them without needing

---

[1] i.e. " as containing discursive principles " (whereas mathematics contains intuitive principles alone).   See pp. 36 and 53.

the mediation of experience or in any way being able to reach them through experience.*

Without a solution to this question reason will never satisfy itself. Use in experience, to which reason limits pure understanding, will not fulfil reason's own complete destiny. Every particular experience is only a part of the whole sphere of the territory of experience ; but the *absolute whole of all possible experience* is not itself experience and yet is a necessary problem for reason. For the mere representation of this problem reason needs concepts quite different from these pure concepts of the understanding, the use of which is only *immanent*, i.e. bears on experience in so far as it can be given. Concepts of reason on the other hand bear on the completeness i.e. the collective unity of all possible experience, thereby going beyond every given experience and becoming *transcendent*.

As the understanding needed categories for experience, so reason contains in itself the ground of ideas, by which I mean necessary concepts, the object of which *can* none the less *not* be given in any experience. Ideas lie in the nature of reason, as categories in the nature of the understanding, and if ideas carry with them an illusion which can easily mislead, this illusion is unavoidable, although " that it shall not seduce into error " can very well be prevented.

As all illusion consists in taking the subjective ground of judgement to be objective, self-knowledge of pure reason in its transcendent (hyperbolical) use will be the only safe-guard against the aberrations into which reason falls when it mistakes its destiny, and refers transcendently to the object in itself that which only concerns reason's own subject and the conduct of it in all its immanent uses.

* If it can be said that a science, at least in the idea of all men, is *real* as soon as it has been established that the problems which lead to it are put before everyone by the nature of human reason, and hence at all times many though faulty essays in it are unavoidable, it will also have to be said that metaphysics is subjectively (indeed necessarily) real ; and then we can legitimately ask how it is (objectively) possible.

§ 41

The distinction of *Ideas*, i.e. of pure concepts of reason, from the categories or pure concepts of the understanding, as knowledge of a quite different kind, origin and use, is so important an item in the grounding of a science which is to contain the system of all this knowledge *a priori*, that without such a separation metaphysics is absolutely impossible or at best an irregular, bungling attempt to build a house of cards without knowledge of the materials with which one is working and of their fitness for one purpose or another. If critique o.p.r. had achieved nothing else than to make this distinction plain for the first time, it would have contributed more to the enlightenment of our comprehension and to the conduct of enquiry in the field of metaphysics than all the fruitless efforts to do justice to the transcendent problems of p. r. that have ever been undertaken ; for it was never even suspected that this was quite another field from that of the understanding, and hence that concepts of the understanding and of reason were being mentioned in the same breath, as if they were of the same kind.

§ 42

All pure knowledge by the understanding has this in common, that its concepts can be given in experience and its principles confirmed by experience ; whereas transcendent knowledge by reason can neither be given, as far as its *ideas* are concerned, in experience, nor its *propositions* ever be confirmed or refuted by experience. Hence the error that may creep in can never be discovered by anything other than pure reason itself, which is very difficult, because this very reason naturally becomes dialectical by means of its ideas, and the illusion which inevitably follows can be held in limits by no objective and dogmatic enquiries into things but merely by subjective enquiries into reason itself as a source of ideas.

§ 43

It was always my highest aim in the Critique to see how I might be able not only carefully to distinguish the kinds of knowledge, but also to deduce all the concepts belonging to each of them from their common source, so that I should not only be able securely to determine their use, being informed about where they were derived from, but also might enjoy the inestimable advantage, never previously anticipated, of knowing completeness in the enumerating, classifying and specifying of the concepts *a priori*, and of knowing it according to principles. Without this everything in metaphysics is nothing but rhapsody, in which one never knows whether one has enough of what one possesses, or whether, and where, something may still be missing. Admittedly this advantage can only be had in pure philosophy, but of this it constitutes the essence.

As I had found the origin of the categories in the four logical functions of all judgements of the understanding, it was quite natural to look for the origin of the ideas in the three functions of syllogisms; because if such pure concepts of reason (transc. ideas) are once given, they might well be encountered, unless they were held to be innate, nowhere else than in the same act of reason which, in so far as it merely concerns the form, constitutes what is logical in syllogisms, but in so far as it represents judgements of the understanding as determined in respect of one or the other form *a priori*, constitutes the transcendental concepts of pure reason.

The formal difference of syllogisms makes their division into categorical, hypothetical, and disjunctive necessary. The concepts of reason grounded thereon thus contain first the idea of the complete subject (the substantial), secondly the idea of the complete series of conditions, and thirdly the determination of all concepts in the idea of a complete totality of the possible.* The first idea was psychological,

---

* In the disjunctive judgement we regard *all possibility* as divided in respect of a certain concept. The ontological principle of the

the second cosmological, the third theological, and as all three give occasion for a dialectic, but each in its own way, they were the ground for the division of the whole dialectic of pure reason : into the paralogism, the antinomy, and finally the ideal of pure reason, through which deduction we are completely assured that all claims of pure reason are here quite completely represented and not a single one can be missing, because the faculty of reason itself from which alone [1] they take their origin is exhaustively surveyed by it.

§ 44

It is further worthy in general of note, while making these considerations : that the ideas of reason are not, like the categories, of any use to us for the employment of the understanding in respect of experience but are entirely dispensable in respect of it, indeed opposed and a hindrance to the maxims of knowledge of nature by reason, although they are necessary to another end that is yet to be determined.   Whether the soul is a simple substance or not, is quite indifferent to us for explaining the appearances of the soul ; for we cannot make the concept of a simple being understandable sensibly and *in concreto* by any possible experience, and thus it is quite empty in respect of all the desired insight into the cause of appearances, and cannot serve as a principle for explaining what inner or outer experience offers.   Nor can we use the cosmological ideas

thoroughgoing determination of a thing in general (of all possible opposite predicates one is attributable to each thing), which is at the same time the principle of all disjunctive judgements, has as its ground the totality of all possibility, in which the possibility of every thing in general is regarded as determinable.   This serves as a little illustration of the above proposition : that the act of reason in disjunctive syllogisms is the same, as to its form, as that through which it brings into being the idea of a totality of all reality, which contains in itself the positive member of all opposite predicates.

[1] Text defective ;   could also be emended to read " from which they all . . .".

of the beginning of the world or of the eternity of the world (*a parte ante*) in order to explain any event in the world itself. Finally, according to a correct maxim of natural philosophy, we must refrain from all explanation of the ordinance of nature drawn from the will of a highest being, because this is no longer natural philosophy but an admission that we are coming to the end of it. These ideas thus have a quite different determination of their use than the categories, through which and through the principles built on them experience itself first became possible. Yet our laborious analytic of the understanding would also be quite superfluous if our aim was directed to nothing other than mere knowledge of nature as it can be given in experience ; for reason does its job quite safely and well both in mathematics and in natural science without all this subtle deduction. Thus our critique of the understanding is linked with the ideas of pure reason to an end which lies beyond the use of the understanding in experience, and we have said above that the use of the understanding in this regard is wholly impossible and without object or meaning. But there must still be agreement between what belongs to the nature of reason and of the understanding, and the former must contribute to the perfection of the latter, and cannot possibly confuse it.

The solution of this question is as follows. Pure reason does not, with its ideas, have as its aim particular objects lying beyond the field of experience, but only demands completeness in the use of the understanding in the complex of experience. This completeness can however only be a completeness of principles, not of intuitions and objects. None the less, in order to represent this completeness to itself determinately and to bring knowledge by the understanding as near as possible to the completeness which this idea denotes, it thinks of it as knowledge of an object, knowledge of which is completely determined in respect of the rules of the understanding, which object is however only an idea.

§ 45

Preliminary Remark
to the

DIALECTIC OF PURE REASON

We have shown above in paragraphs 33 and 34 : that the purity of the categories from all admixture of sensible determinations can mislead reason into extending their use quite beyond all experience to things in themselves ; whereas, categories being merely logical functions and finding no intuition themselves which could provide them with meaning and sense *in concreto*, they can give no determinate concept of anything at all by themselves, even though they can represent a thing in general. Such hyperbolical objects are what are called *noumena* or pure beings of the understanding (or better, beings of thought), as for example, *substance*, but thought *without permanence* in time, or a *cause*, but *not* acting *in time*, etc. To these objects predicates are attributed which can only serve to make possible the conformity of experience to law, and yet all conditions of intuition, under which alone experience is possible, are taken away from them, whereby these concepts lose all meaning again.

There is no danger that the understanding will wander of itself quite so wantonly beyond its own boundaries into the field of mere beings of the understanding, without being impelled by alien laws. But reason can never be completely satisfied by any use of the rules of the understanding in experience, this use always remaining conditioned ; and when reason demands completion of this chain of conditions, it drives the understanding out of its sphere, partly to represent objects of experience in a series so far extended that no experience whatever can comprehend it, partly even (in order to complete it), to seek *noumena* quite outside experience, to which the chain can be fastened ; whereby reason, independent at long last of the conditions of experience, can nevertheless make its hold complete. These are then the transcendental ideas which, even though they aim, not at extravagant concepts, but according to the true but hidden end of the natural determination of our reason merely at the unlimited extension of use in experience, yet through an unavoidable illusion entice from the understanding a *transcendent* use which, although deceptive, cannot be kept in limits by a resolve to stay within the bounds of experience, but only by scientific instruction and taking pains.

I.   Psychological Idea
(Critique p. 341 f.) [1]

§ 46

It has long since been noticed that in all substances the subject proper, namely what is left over after all accidents (as predicates) have been taken away and hence the *substantial* itself, is unknown to us, and diverse complaints have been made about these limits of our insight.   But it must be noted well that the human understanding is not to be blamed for not knowing, i.e. not being able to determine by itself, the substantial in things, but for demanding to know it determinately like a given object, it being a mere idea.   Pure reason demands that for every predicate of a thing we should look for its appropriate subject, and for this, which is necessarily in its turn only a predicate, its subject and so on to infinity (or as far as we can reach). But it follows from this that nothing which we can reach ought to be taken as a final subject, and that the substantial itself can never be thought by our understanding, however deeply it penetrated, and even if the whole of nature were disclosed to it ; because the specific nature of our understanding consists in thinking everything discursively, i.e. through concepts, and hence through nothing but predicates to which the absolute subject must always be lacking.

[1] i.e. A341/B399, Of the Paralogisms of Pure Reason.

Hence all real properties through which we know bodies are nothing but accidents, even impenetrability, which one must always represent to oneself only as the effect of a force of which we do not have the subject.

Now it seems as if we have something that is substantial, and an immediate intuition of it, in the consciousness of ourself (i.e. in the thinking subject) ; for all predicates of inner sense refer to the *I* as subject, and this cannot be thought further as the predicate of any other subject.   Here therefore completeness in the reference of given concepts as predicates to a subject seems to be not merely an idea, but the object, namely the *absolute subject* itself, seems to be given in experience.   But this expectation comes to nothing. For the I is not a concept *, but only a designation of the object of inner sense in so far as we know it through no further predicate ; and though it cannot in itself be the predicate of another thing, it also cannot be a determinate concept of an absolute subject, but only, as in all other cases, the reference of inner appearances to the unknown subject of them.   Nevertheless this idea (which, as a regulative principle, serves very well wholly to destroy all materialistic explanations of the inner appearances of our soul) is through a quite natural misunderstanding the occasion of a very specious argument which infers the nature of our thinking being, in so far as knowledge of it falls quite outside the totality of experience, from this supposed knowledge of the substantial in it.

§ 47

This thinking self (the soul) may indeed be called substance, as the last subject of thinking which cannot itself

---

* If the representation of apperception, the I, were a concept through which anything was thought, it could also be used as predicate of other things or contain such predicates in itself. But it is nothing more than feeling of an existence without the slightest concept, and only representation of an that to which all thinking stands in relation (*relatione accidentis*).[1]

[1] "in the relation of accident ".

be further represented as predicate of any other thing ; but even so this concept remains wholly empty and without any consequences, unless it can be proved to have permanence, which is what makes the concept of substances fruitful in experience.

Permanence can only be proved on behalf of experience, never out of the concept of a substance as a thing in itself. This has been adequately shown in the first analogy of experience (Critique p. 182),[1] and anyone who does not accept this proof may make the attempt himself and see whether he succeeds in proving from the concept of a subject which does not itself exist as predicate of another thing that its existence is thoroughly permanent and that it can neither come into being nor pass away of itself or through any natural cause. Such synthetic propositions *a priori* can never be proved in themselves, but only with reference to things as objects of a possible experience.

§ 48

If therefore we want to infer permanence of the soul from the concept of the soul as substance, this can only be valid of it for the sake of possible experience, and not valid of it as a thing in itself and beyond all possible experience. Now the subjective condition of all our possible experience is life ; consequently only the permanence of the soul in life can be inferred, for the death of man is the end of all experience, so far as the soul as an object of experience is concerned, except the contrary, which however is in question, be shown. Thus the permanence of the soul can only be shown in the life of man (the proof of which may be allowed us) but not after death (which is what we are properly concerned with), and this on the universal ground that the concept of substance, in so far as it is to be regarded as necessarily joined with the concept of permanence, can only be so joined according to a principle of pos-

[1] i.e. A182/B224.

sible experience and therefore only for the sake of
experience.*

§ 49

That something real outside us not merely corresponds
but must correspond to our outer perceptions can likewise
never be proved as a connection of things in themselves,
but can well be for the sake of experience.   This is as much
as to say : it can very well be proved that something is
outside us in an empirical way, and as appearance in space ;
for we are not concerned with objects other than those which
belong to a possible experience, precisely because they can
be given to us in no experience and so for us are nothing.
What is intuited in space is empirically outside me, and
as this together with all the appearances that it contains
belongs to representations, the connection of which according to laws of experience proves their objective truth
equally as the connection of appearances of inner sense

* It is in fact very remarkable that metaphysicians have always
slipped over the principle of the permanence of substances in so carefree
a way, without ever attempting a proof of it ; doubtless because, as soon
as they set to work on the concept of substance, they found themselves
wholly abandoned by all arguments.   Common sense, which was well
aware that without this presupposition no unification of perceptions in
a consciousness was possible, made up for this defect by a postulate ;
for it could never have drawn this principle from experience itself,
partly because it cannot follow materials (substances) in all their
changes and dissolutions far enough always to find the matter undimin-
ished, partly because the principle contains *necessity*, which is always
the sign of a principle *a priori*.   Now it confidently applied this principle
to the concept of a soul as a *substance*, and inferred a necessary continu-
ance of the soul after the death of man (especially because the simple-
ness of this substance which was inferred from the indivisibility of consciousness secured it against disappearance through dissolution).   If
these metaphysicians had found the genuine source of this principle,
which demanded far deeper enquiries than they were ever inclined to
begin, they would have seen : that this law of the permanence of substances only finds a place for the sake of experience, and hence can
only be valid for things in so far as they are to be known in experience
and joined with others, but never for them regardless of all possible
experience, and hence not for the soul after death.

proves the reality of my soul (as an object of inner sense), I am conscious equally by means of outer experience of the reality of bodies as outer appearances in space, as of the existence of my soul in time by means of inner experience. I know my soul only as an object of inner sense, by appearances which constitute an inner state, and the essence of it in itself which lies at the ground of these appearances is unknown to me. Cartesian idealism thus only distinguishes outer experience from dreams, and conformity to law as a criterion of the truth of the former from the irregularity and false illusion of the latter. In both it presupposes space and time as conditions of the existence of objects, and only asks whether the objects of the outer senses that we place in space in waking are really to be found there, as the object of inner sense, the soul, is really in time, i.e. whether experience carries with it sure criteria for distinguishing it from imagination. This doubt can easily be overcome, and we overcome it all the time in ordinary life by enquiring into the connection of appearances in both according to universal laws of experience, and cannot doubt that the representation of outer things, if it is in thoroughgoing agreement with them, should constitute true experience. Material idealism, in which appearances as appearances are only considered according to their connection in experience, can very easily be overcome, and it is just as sure an experience that bodies exist outside us (in space) as that I myself exist according to the representation of inner sense (in time). For the concept *outside us* only means existence in space. But the I in the proposition *I am* means not merely the object of inner intuition (in time) but also the subject of consciousness, as body means not merely the outer intuition (in space) but also the thing *in itself* that lies at the ground of this appearance ; and therefore the question whether bodies (as appearances of outer sense) exist *outside my thoughts* as bodies in nature can be answered without any hesitation in the negative ; but the same is also the case with the question whether I myself *as appearance of inner sense* (soul according to empirical psychology) exist in time outside my faculty of representation, for this must also be answered in the negative. In this way everything is decided, and with certainty, when it is brought to its true meaning. Formal idealism (otherwise called by me transcendental idealism) really overcomes the material or Cartesian idealism. For if space is nothing but a form of my sensibility, it is just as real, as representation in me, as I am myself, and it is only a question of the empirical truth of appearances in it. If it is not, and if space and appearances in it are something existing outside us, then all criteria of experience outside our perception can never prove the reality of these objects outside us.

II. Cosmological Ideas
(Critique p. 405 f.) [1]

§ 50

This product of pure reason in its transcendent use is the most remarkable phenomenon of it, and also has the most powerful effect of all in waking philosophy out of its dogmatic slumber and urging it to the arduous task of the critique of reason itself.

I call this idea cosmological because it always takes its object only from the world of the senses and needs none other than those,[2] the object of which is an object of the senses, and thus far is immanent and not transcendent, consequently is not as yet an idea ; whereas on the contrary to think the soul as a simple substance is already as much as to think an object (the simple) such as cannot be represented to the senses. Notwithstanding, the cosmological idea extends the connection of the conditioned with its condition (whether mathematical or dynamic) so far that experience can never come equal to it, and thus is still in

---

[1] i.e. A405/B432, The Antinomy of Pure Reason.

[2] Attribution of this pronoun obscure ; perhaps " representations " (cf. 4 lines below) is intended.

respect of this point an idea the object of which can never be adequately given in any experience.

§ 51

In the first place the utility of a system of categories shows itself here so clearly and unmistakably that even if there were not several other proofs of it this alone would adequately show its indispensability in the system of pure reason. There are no more than four such transcendent ideas, as many as there are classes of the categories ; but in each of them they only bear on the absolute completeness of the series of conditions for something that is given as conditioned. In conformity with these cosmological ideas there are also only four kinds of dialectical assertions of pure reason, which themselves prove by their being dialectical that to each of them a contradictory one is opposed, according to equally specious principles of pure reason, which contradiction can be prevented by no metaphysical art of the most subtle distinction, but compels the philosopher to go back to the first sources of pure reason itself. This antinomy, not arbitrarily invented but grounded in the nature of human reason, and hence unavoidable and never-ending, contains [*overleaf*] the following four propositions together with their opposites :

§ 52

Here we have the strangest phenomenon of human reason, no other example of which can be indicated in any other use of reason. If, as usually happens, we think of the appearances of the world of the senses as things in themselves, if we take the principles of their connection as principles universally valid of things in themselves and not merely valid of experience, as is equally usual, indeed without our critique unavoidable, an unsuspected conflict appears, which can never be removed in the usual dogmatic way, because both thesis and antithesis can be established by equally evident, clear and irresistible proofs —for I pledge myself for the correctness of all these proofs—

[§ 51, table]

1.

THESIS
The world, as to time and space, has
a beginning (*boundary*)

ANTITHESIS
The world, as to time and space, is
infinite

2.

THESIS
Everything in the world is constituted out of the
simple

ANTITHESIS
There is nothing simple, but everything is
composite

3.

THESIS
There are in the world causes through
freedom

ANTITHESIS
There is no freedom, but everything is
nature

4.

THESIS
In the series of causes of the world there is some
necessary being

ANTITHESIS
There is nothing necessary in it, but in this series
everything is contingent

and reason thus sees itself divided against itself, a state at which the sceptic rejoices but which must cause the critical philosopher reflection and disquiet.

§ 52b

It is possible to blunder around in metaphysics in many ways, without fear of being detected in falsehood. For we have only not to contradict ourselves, which is very well possible in synthetic though wholly fictitious propositions; and in all cases in which the concepts that we connect are mere ideas which can never (as to their whole content) be given in experience, we can never be refuted by experience. For how should we decide by experience whether the world exists from eternity or has a beginning, or whether matter is infinitely divisible or consists of simple parts. Such concepts cannot be given even in the greatest possible experience, and the incorrectness of the thesis asserted or denied cannot be discovered by this touchstone.

The only possible case in which reason would reveal against its will its secret dialectic, which it falsely gives out as dogma, would be that in which it grounded an assertion on a universally conceded principle, and inferred exactly the opposite from another equally well attested principle, with the greatest correctness of argument. Here we have this case in reality, in respect of four natural ideas of reason, from which there arise on the one hand four assertions and on the other hand as many counter-assertions each argued in correct consequence from universally admitted principles, thus revealing the dialectical illusion of pure reason in the use of these principles, which otherwise would have had to remain eternally hidden.

This is therefore a crucial experiment which must necessarily discover to us an incorrectness that lies hidden in the presuppositions of reason.* Of two contradictory proposi-

* I should therefore like the critical reader [1] to concern himself mainly with this antinomy, because nature itself seems to have arranged

---

[1] Reader of the *Critique of Pure Reason*.

tions both cannot be false, unless the concept that lies at the ground of both of them is self-contradictory. For example, the two propositions : a four-cornered circle is round, and a four-cornered circle is not round, are both false.   For as concerns the first it is false that the said circle is round, because it is four-cornered ; but it is also false that it is not round, i.e. has corners, because it is a circle. For the logical mark of the impossibility of a concept consists precisely in this, that when it is presupposed two contradictory propositions are both false, and as no third proposition can be thought between them, *nothing whatever* can be thought through that concept.

§ 52c

The two first antinomies, which I call mathematical because they are concerned with the addition or division of the homogeneous, have such a contradictory concept as their ground, and from this I explain how it happens that thesis as well as antithesis are false in both.

If I speak of objects in space and time, I do not speak of things in themselves because I know nothing about them, but only of things in appearance, i.e. of experience as a particular way of knowing objects which is vouchsafed to man alone.   I must not say, of what I think in space and time, that in itself and without these my thoughts it is in space and time ; for I should then be contradicting myself; because space and time, together with appearances in them, are nothing existing in themselves and outside my representations, but are themselves only modes of representation,

---

it to make reason stop short in its bold pretensions and to compel it to self-examination.   I pledge myself to be responsible for every proof which I have given for the thesis as well as for the antithesis, and thereby to show the certainty of the unavoidable antinomy of reason.   If the reader is persuaded by this strange phenomenon to go back to test the presupposition lying at its ground, he will feel himself constrained to enquire more deeply with me into the first basis of all knowledge of pure reason.

and it is manifestly contradictory to say that a mere mode of representation also exists outside our representation. Thus the objects of the senses exist only in experience ; whereas to give them their own existence in themselves, without experience or prior to it, is as much as to represent experience as also being real without experience or prior to it.

If I ask about the size of the world, as to space and time, it is for all my concepts equally impossible to say that it is infinite as that it is finite. For neither can be contained in experience, because experience is possible neither of an *infinite* space nor of infinite time elapsed, nor of the *bounding* of the world by an empty space or by a previous empty time ; these are only ideas. This size of the world, determined in one way or another, would have to lie in the world itself, separately from all experience. But this contradicts the concept of a world of the senses, which is only a totality of appearance, the existence and connection of which only finds a place in representation, namely in experience, because it is not a thing in itself but is itself nothing but a mode of representation. It follows from this that as the concept of a world of the senses existing for itself is contradictory within itself, the solution to the problem of its size would always be false, whether attempted positively or negatively.

The same holds of the second antinomy which concerns the division of appearances. For these are mere representations and the parts exist merely in the representation of them and in division, i.e. in a possible experience in which they are given, and hence the division only goes so far as experience reaches. To assume that an appearance, e.g. that of a body, contains in itself before all experience all parts to which any possible experience whatever can reach, means : to give to a mere appearance, which can only exist in experience, an existence of its own preceding experience, or to say that mere representations are there before they are encountered in the faculty of representation, which is self-contradictory; as is also every solution of this misunderstood problem, whether it is asserted that bodies consist in themselves of an infinite number of parts or of a finite number of simple parts.

§ 53

In the first class of the antinomy (the mathematical) the falsehood of the presupposition consisted in representing what is self-contradictory (namely appearance as thing in itself) as compatible in a concept. As concerns the second, namely the dynamic class of the antinomy, the falsehood of the presupposition consists in representing what is compatible as contradictory. Consequently whereas in the first case both the opposing assertions were false, in this case those that are opposed to each other by mere misunderstanding can both be true.

Mathematical connection necessarily presupposes homogeneity in what is connected (in the concept of size), dynamic connection does not in any way demand this. If it is a matter of the size of the extended, all the parts must be homogeneous among themselves and with the whole; whereas in the connection of cause and effect homogeneity may also be found, but it is not necessary; for the concept of causality (by means of which something is posited through something quite different from it) at least does not demand it.

If the objects of the world of the senses were taken for things in themselves, and the above-quoted laws of nature for laws of things in themselves, the contradiction would be unavoidable. Equally, if the subject of freedom were represented as mere appearance, like other objects, the contradiction could also not be avoided, for the same thing would be simultaneously affirmed and denied of the same object in the same meaning. But if natural necessity is referred merely to appearances, and freedom merely to things in themselves, no contradiction arises, if one assumes or admits at the same time both kinds of causality, however difficult or impossible it may be to make the latter kind of causality conceivable.

In appearance, every effect is an event, or something that happens in time; according to the universal law of nature it must be preceded by a determination of the causality of the thing that is its cause (a state of the cause) on which the effect follows according to a constant law. But this determination of the cause to causality [1] must also be something *that* occurs or *happens*; the cause must have *begun to act*, for otherwise no sequence in time between the cause and the effect could be thought. The effect would have always existed, as also the causality of the cause. Thus the *determination* of the cause *to act* must have arisen among appearances and must also, as well as its effect, be an event, which must have its cause in its turn, and so on, and consequently natural necessity must be the condition according to which effective causes are determined. But if freedom is to be a property of certain causes of appearances, it must be, with respect to the latter as events, a faculty of beginning them *of itself* (*sponte*), i.e. without the causality of the cause itself needing to begin, and hence needing no other ground determining its beginning. But then *the cause*, as to its causality, would not have to stand under time-determinations of its state, i.e. *not be appearance* at all, i.e. it would have to be taken as a thing in itself, but the *effects* would have to be taken only as *appearances*.* If

* The idea of freedom finds a place solely in the relation of the *intellectual* as cause to the *appearance* as effect. Hence we cannot attribute freedom to matter in respect of its unceasing activity through which it fills its space, although this activity happens out of an inner principle. Nor can we find a concept of freedom appropriate to pure beings of the understanding, e.g. God, in so far as his activity is immanent. For his activity, although independent of outer determining causes, is yet determined in his eternal reason and in the divine *nature*. Only when *something* is to *begin* through an act and the effect is to be encountered in the time sequence, consequently in the world of the senses (e.g. the beginning of the world), does the question arise,

[1] i.e. causation, active causing.

one can think such an influence of beings of the understanding on appearances without contradiction, natural necessity will indeed inhere in all connection of cause and effect in the world of the senses, but freedom will have to be conceded to that cause which is not itself appearance (although it lies at the ground of appearance) ; nature and freedom will be capable of being attributed without contradiction to the same thing, but in a different reference, on the one hand to it as appearance, on the other to it as a thing in itself.

We have within us a faculty which is not merely connected with its subjectively determining grounds, namely the natural causes of its acts, and thus far the faculty of a being which itself belongs to appearances, but also has objective grounds which are merely ideas, to which it is related in that they are able to determine this faculty. This connection is expressed by *ought*. This faculty is called *reason*, and when we consider a being (man) solely with regard to this objectively determinable reason, he cannot be considered as a being of the senses ; the said property, being the property of a thing in itself, is one the possibility of which we cannot conceive, namely how the *ought*, which has never been the case, should determine its activity and could be the cause of acts, the effect of which is appearance in the world of the senses.   Yet the causality of reason [1] would be freedom in respect of effects in the world of the senses, in so far as *objective grounds* which are themselves ideas are regarded as determining in respect of it.   For its act would not then depend on subjective conditions, nor on time-conditions and thus also not on the law whether the causality of the cause must also itself begin or whether the cause can start an effect without its causality itself beginning.   In the first case the concept of this causality is a concept of natural necessity, in the second case of freedom.   The reader will see from this that when I explained freedom as the faculty of beginning an event spontaneously, I exactly hit the concept which is the problem of metaphysics.

---

[1] i.e. causation by reason.

of nature that serves to determine these conditions, because grounds of reason give a rule to actions universally, from principles, without influence from the circumstances of time and place.

What I am adducing here only holds as an example, for intelligibility, and does not belong necessarily to our question which must be decided out of mere concepts, independently of the properties which we encounter in the real world.

I can now say without contradiction : all acts of rational beings, in that they are appearances (are encountered in some experience), stand under natural necessity ; the same acts however, merely with respect to the rational subject and to its faculty of acting according to mere reason, are free. For what is demanded for natural necessity ? Nothing further than the determinability of every event in the world of the senses according to constant laws and a reference to a cause in appearance, while the thing in itself that lies at the ground and its causality remain unknown. But I say : *the law of nature stands*, whether the rational being is the cause, by reason and through freedom, of effects in the world of the senses, or whether it does not determine these effects out of grounds of reason. For in the first case the act happens according to maxims the effect of which in appearance will always be in conformity with constant laws ; in the second case, the act happening not according to principles of reason, it is subject to the empirical laws of sensibility, and in both cases the effects are connected according to constant laws ; we demand no more for natural necessity, indeed we know nothing more of it. But in the first case reason is the cause of these natural laws and is thus free, in the second case the effects run according to mere natural laws of sensibility because reason exercises no influence on them ; but reason itself is not thus determined by sensibility (which is impossible) and hence is free in this case also. Freedom thus hinders the natural law of appearances by as little as the natural law takes away from the freedom of the practical use of reason which is connected with things in themselves as its determining grounds.

This rescues practical freedom, namely that in which reason has causality according to objectively determining grounds, without the least loss to natural necessity in respect of the same effects taken as appearances. This can also serve to illustrate what we had to say about transcendental freedom and its compatibility with natural necessity (in the same subject, but not taken in one and the same reference). For as far as this is concerned, every beginning of an act of a being from objective causes is always, in respect of these determining grounds, a *first beginning*, although in the series of appearances the same act is only a *subordinate beginning* which must be preceded by a state of the cause which determines it and which is itself determined by another immediately preceding ; so that for rational beings, or for beings in general, the causality of which is determined in them as things in themselves, we can think a faculty of beginning of themselves a series of states, without running into contradiction with natural laws. For the relation of the act to objective grounds of reason is not a time-relation ; what determines the causality does not precede the act in time, because such determining grounds do not represent reference of objects to senses, and hence not to causes in appearance, but represent determining causes as things in themselves which do not stand under time-conditions. Thus the act can be regarded as a first beginning in respect of the causality of reason, and at the same time as a merely subordinate beginning in respect of the series of appearances, and can be regarded without contradiction as free in the former respect and in the latter (as it is merely appearance) as subordinated to natural necessity.

As concerns the *fourth* antinomy, this is overcome in the same way as the conflict of reason with itself in the third. For if only the *cause in appearance* is distinguished from *the cause of appearances*, in so far as it can be thought as a *thing in itself*, both propositions can well stand side by side, namely that in the world of the senses no cause at all, the existence of which is absolutely necessary, finds a place (according to similar laws of causality), yet on the other hand that this world is connected with a necessary being as its cause (but of a different kind and according to a different law) ; the incompatibility of which two propositions rests solely on the misunderstanding of extending what is valid merely of appearances to things in themselves, and in general mixing the two in one concept.

§ 54

This is the setting up and solution of the whole antinomy in which reason finds itself involved when it applies its principles to the world of the senses. Even the mere setting up of it would alone be a considerable service to knowledge of human reason, even if the reader should not yet be entirely satisfied by the solution of this conflict, having to fight against a natural illusion which has only recently been represented to him as such, after he had always previously taken it for true. For one consequence of this is inevitable, namely that because it is quite impossible to emerge from this conflict of reason with itself so long as the objects of the world of the senses are taken for things in themselves and not for what they in fact are, namely mere appearances, the reader will be compelled to undertake once more the deduction of all our knowledge *a priori* and the examination of the deduction which I have given, in order to come to a decision about it. I do not ask more at present ; for if in doing this he has once thought himself deeply enough into the nature of pure reason, the concepts through which alone the solution of the conflict of reason is possible will be familiar to him, without which circumstance I cannot expect complete assent even from the most attentive reader.

III.   Theological Idea
(Critique p. 571 f.)[1]

§ 55

The third transcendental idea, which provides material for that use of reason which is the most important of all, but which, if pursued merely speculatively, is a hyperbolical (transcendent) and thereby dialectical use of it, is the ideal of pure reason.   Reason does not here start from experience, as with the psychological and cosmological idea, to be misled into striving after a would-be absolute completion of the series of its grounds by going to ever higher ones. Here on the contrary reason breaks off completely and descends from mere concepts of what would constitute the absolute completeness of a thing in general, by means of the idea of a most perfect original being, to the determina- tion of the possibility and also of the reality of all other things.   Hence the mere presupposition of a being which, although not in the series of experiences, is thought on behalf of experience and for the sake of the conceivability of the connection, order and unity of it, i.e. the *idea*, is easier to distinguish here from the concept of the under- standing, than in the previous cases.   Hence the dialectical illusion which arises from taking the subjective conditions of our thought for objective conditions of the things them- selves and taking a hypothesis necessary to the satisfaction of our reason for a dogma, could easily be made plain, and hence I have nothing further to remark about the pre- tensions of transcendental theology, as what the Critique says about this is easily grasped, clear and decisive.

§ 56

General Note to the Transcendental Ideas

The objects which are given to us by experience are from many points of view inconceivable, and many ques-

---

[1] i.e. A571/B599, Of the transcendental Ideal.

tions to which the law of nature leads us, when they are driven to a certain height but still in conformity with these laws, cannot be solved at all ; for instance whence matter has its mutual attraction. But if we go outside nature completely or in the course of its connection overstep all possible experience and submerge ourselves in mere ideas, we cannot then say that the object is inconceivable for us and that the nature of things presents us with insoluble problems ; for we then have to do, not with nature or with given objects at all, but merely with concepts which have their origin solely in our reason, and with mere beings of thought in respect of which all problems which arise out of the concept of them must be capable of being solved, because reason certainly can and must give complete justification for its own process.* As the psychological, cosmological and theological ideas are nothing but pure concepts of reason, which cannot be given in any experience, the questions which reason presents to us in respect of them are offered not through objects but through mere maxims of reason for the sake of its own self-satisfaction and must all be capable of being adequately answered. This is done by showing that they are principles for establishing thoroughgoing unanimity, completeness and synthetic unity in the use of our understanding, and hence that

---

* Hence Herr Platner [1] acutely says in his Aphorisms, §§ 728, 729 : " If reason is a criterion, no concept can be possible which is inconceivable to human reason. . . . In reality alone does inconceivability find its place. Here the inconceivability arises out of the inadequacy of acquired ideas."—Thus it only sounds paradoxical and is not in any other way strange to say that in nature much is inconceivable to us (e.g. the faculty of generation), but if we rise higher and even go beyond nature everything will become conceivable again ; for then we completely leave *objects* which can be given to us, and occupy ourselves merely with ideas, and here we can well conceive the law which reason prescribes through them to the understanding for its use in experience, because it is reason's own product.

---

[1] Ernst Platner (1744–1818) : *Philosophische Aphorismen* 2 vols., Leipzig, 1776–82.

they are valid merely of experience, but of the *whole* of it. But although an absolute whole of experience is impossible, the idea of a whole of knowledge according to principles in general is what alone can procure for it a special kind of unity, namely that of a system, without which our experience is nothing but patchwork and cannot be used for the highest end (which is always only the system of all ends) ; and here I mean not merely the practical use of reason, but also the highest end of the speculative use of reason.

The transcendental ideas thus express the peculiar destiny of reason as a principle of the systematic unity of the use of the understanding. But if this unity of the way of knowing is regarded as if it inhered in the object of knowledge, if, properly being merely *regulative*, it is taken to be *constitutive*, and one persuades oneself that by means of these ideas knowledge can be extended far beyond all possible experience, in a transcendent way, whereas it merely serves to bring experience as near as possible to completeness within itself, i.e. not to limit its progress by anything that cannot belong to experience, all this is a mere misunderstanding in judging the proper destiny of our reason and its principles, and a dialectic which partly confuses the use of reason in experience, partly divides reason against itself.

CONCLUSION

OF THE DETERMINATION OF THE BOUNDARIES OF PURE REASON

§ 57

After the clearest of all proofs, which we have given above, it would be an absurdity to hope to know more of any object than belongs to possible experience of it, or to claim the least knowledge of how anything that we take not to be an object of possible experience is determined as to what it is like in itself. For how are we to make this determination, when time, space and all concepts of the understanding, and even more so the concepts drawn from empirical intuition or *perception* in the world of the senses, have and can have no other use than merely to make experience possible; and if we leave out this condition, even from the pure concepts of the understanding, they at once cease to determine any object whatever, and have no meaning at all?

But it would be an even greater absurdity on the other hand to admit no things in themselves, or to declare our experience to be the only possible way of knowing things, our intuition in space and time the only possible intuition, our discursive understanding the archetype of every possible understanding, and to have the principles of the possibility of experience taken for universal conditions of things in themselves.

Our principles, which limit the use of reason merely to possible experience, could accordingly themselves become *transcendent*, and declare the limits of our reason to be limits of the possibility of things themselves, of which HUME's Dialogues [1] may serve as an example, if a careful critique did not watch the boundaries of our reason in respect also of its empirical use and set a term to its claims. Scepticism arose originally out of metaphysics and the lawlessness of its dialectic. At first scepticism may have merely declared, in favour of the use of reason in experience, that everything that transcends this is null and deceptive; but gradually, as it was seen that the same principles *a priori*, which are used in experience, imperceptibly and as it seemed with equal right led further than experience reaches, doubt began to be placed even in principles of experience. There is no danger in this, for common sense will always assert its rights in experience, but there arose

---

[1] Hume: *Dialogues concerning Natural Religion* (1779), German translation, Leipzig, 1781.

a strange confusion in science, which cannot determine how far reason is to be trusted, and why only so far and no further. This confusion can only be removed, and all future relapses prevented, by formal determination, drawn from principles, of the boundaries of the use of our reason.

It is true: we can give no determinate concept of what things may be in themselves beyond all possible experience. But we are not free to refrain completely from enquiry after them; for experience is never entirely enough for reason. In answering questions it always points further and further back and leaves us unsatisfied in respect of their complete solution; the dialectic of pure reason, which precisely because of this has its good subjective ground, enables everyone to see this adequately. Who can bear, as regards the nature of the soul, being able to reach clear consciousness of the subject and also the conviction that its appearances cannot be explained *materialistically*, without asking what the soul properly is; and if no concept of experience gives an adequate answer, who can bear to do no more than assume merely for this purpose a concept of reason (a simple immaterial being), although we cannot show its objective reality? Who can be satisfied with mere knowledge by experience in all cosmological questions of the size and duration of the world, of freedom or natural necessity, since however we go about it every answer given according to fundamental laws of experience [1] always gives birth to a new question, which also demands an answer, and thus clearly shows the inadequacy of all physical kinds of explanation to satisfy reason? Finally, who does not see the impossibility of stopping at the thoroughgoing contingency and dependency of everything that he can think and assume according to principles of experience alone, and does not feel himself compelled, despite all prohibitions not to lose himself in transcendent ideas, to

[1] It has been plausibly proposed that "fundamental laws of experience" should be emended to "principles of experience" (as 6 lines below).

seek peace and satisfaction, beyond all concepts which he can justify by experience, in the concept of a being of which the idea in itself is such that there can indeed be no insight into its possibility, although it also cannot be refuted, because it concerns a mere being of the understanding, but without this idea reason would have to remain for ever unsatisfied?

Boundaries (in extended beings) always presuppose a space which is found outside a certain determined place and encloses it; limits do not need any such thing but are mere negations which affect a quantity in so far as it does not have absolute completeness. But our reason sees so to speak around it a space for knowledge of things in themselves, although it can never have determined concepts of them and is limited merely to experience.

As long as knowledge by reason is homogeneous, no determinate boundaries of it can be thought. In mathematics and natural science human reason recognises limits, but no boundaries; i.e. it recognises that something lies outside it, to which it can never reach, but not that it will ever be completed itself anywhere in its inner progress. The enlargement of insight in mathematics and the possibility of new inventions extends to infinity; equally the discovery of new properties of nature, new forces and laws, by continued experience and unification of it by reason. But none the less we must not fail to see limits here, for mathematics only bears on *appearances*, and what cannot be an object of sensible intuition, such as the concepts of metaphysics and morals, lies quite outside its sphere; mathematics can never lead to it, but also has no need of it. There is therefore a continuous progress and approach to these sciences, and as it were a point or line·of contact. Natural science will never discover to us the inside of things, i.e. that which is not appearance but can serve as the highest ground of explanation of appearances; but natural science does not need this for its physical explanations; indeed if such were offered to it from elsewhere (e.g. influence of immaterial beings), it ought to refuse it and not to bring it in to advance its explanations, but always ground them on what belongs to experience as object of the senses and can be brought into connection with our real perceptions according to laws of experience.

But metaphysics, in the dialectical essays of pure reason (which we do not undertake arbitrarily or wantonly, but are driven to them by the nature of reason itself), leads us to boundaries ; and the transcendental ideas, because there can be no commerce with them and also because they can never be realised, serve not only really to show us the boundaries of the use of pure reason but also the way to determine them ; and that is the end and utility of this natural disposition of our reason which has borne metaphysics as its favourite child whose generation, like every other in the world, is not to be attributed to unforeseen accident but to an original germ which is wisely organised for great ends. For metaphysics, perhaps more than any other science, is laid in us in its fundamental lines by nature itself, and cannot be regarded as the product of an arbitrary choice or an accidental expansion during the advance of experiences (from which it is wholly separate).

Reason, with all its concepts and laws of the understanding which are adequate to it in empirical use and inside the world of the senses, finds no satisfaction in them of itself ; for questions recurring to infinity take away from it all hope of a complete solution of them. The transcendental ideas, which have this completion as their aim, are such problems of reason. Now reason sees clearly : that the world of the senses cannot contain this completion, nor can all those concepts which serve solely for understanding the world of the senses : space and time and everything that we have mentioned under the name of pure concepts of the understanding. The world of the senses is nothing but a chain of appearances connected according to universal laws, it thus has no existence for itself, it is properly not the thing in itself, and thus refers necessarily to that which contains the ground of these appearances, to beings which can be known not merely as appearance, but as things in themselves. In knowledge of these alone can reason ever hope to see its demand for completeness in the advance from the conditioned to its conditions satisfied.

We have indicated above (§§ 33, 34) limits of reason in respect of all knowledge of mere beings of thought ; now, as the transcendental ideas still make the advance to them necessary for us, and have led us as it were only to the contact of filled space (experience) with empty space (of which we can know nothing, the noumena), we can also determine the boundaries of pure reason ; for in all boundaries there is also something positive, (e.g. surface is the boundary of bodily space, but is itself a space ; line is a space which is the boundary of surface, point the boundary of line but still a place in space) ; whereas limits contain mere negations. The limits indicated in the above-mentioned paragraphs are not yet enough, since we have found that something lies beyond them (even though we shall never know it for what it is in itself). For the question now arises, how does our reason behave in this connecting of what we know with that which we do not know and shall never know ? There is here a real connection of the known with a completely unknown (which will always remain so), and even if the unknown is not to become the least bit better known—which cannot in fact be hoped for—the concept of this connection must be capable of being determined and brought to clarity.

We are therefore to think an immaterial being, a world of the understanding and a highest of all beings (nothing but noumena), because only in these, as things in themselves, does reason find the completion and satisfaction which it can never hope for in the deduction of appearances from grounds homogeneous with them ; and because appearances really refer to something different from themselves (and wholly heterogeneous) in that they always presuppose a thing in itself and thus give notice of it, whether it is nown any further or not.

As we can never know these beings of the understanding for what they are in themselves, i.e. determinately, but none the less must assume such beings in relation to the world of the senses and connect them with it by reason, we shall at least be able to think this connection by means of such concepts as express their relation to the world of the senses. For if we think a being of the understanding through nothing but pure concepts of the understanding, we really think nothing determinate and our concept is without meaning; if we think it through properties borrowed from the world of the senses, it is no longer a being of the understanding but is thought as one of the phenomena and belongs to the world of the senses. We shall take as an example the concept of the highest being.

The *Deistic* concept is a wholly pure concept of reason, but one which only represents a thing that contains all reality, without being able to determine one single reality, because to do so the example would have to be taken from the world of the senses, in which case I should still only have to do with an object of the senses and not with something quite heterogeneous which cannot be an object of the senses. For let us suppose for example that I were to attribute to it understanding: but I have no concept of an understanding except of one that is like mine, namely such that intuitions have to be given to it through senses, and that occupies itself with bringing them under rules of the unity of consciousness. But then the elements of my concept would still lie in appearance; but it was the inadequacy of appearances that compelled me to go beyond them to the concept of a being not dependent on appearances or involved with them as conditions of its determination. Yet if I separate the understanding from sensibility in order to have a pure understanding, nothing is left over but the mere form of thought without intuition, through which alone I can know nothing determinate and thus no object. To this end I should have to think a different understanding which intuited objects, but of this I cannot in the least conceive, because the human understanding is discursive and can only know through universal concepts. The same will befall me if I attribute to the highest being a will; for I only have this concept by drawing it from my inner experience, when it remains grounded in our dependence for satisfaction on objects the existence of which we need, and thus in sensibility, which wholly contradicts the pure concept of the highest being.

HUME's objections to deism are weak, and never touch anything more than the arguments, never the proposition of the deistic assertion itself. But in respect of theism, which is supposed to come into being by a closer determination of our concept of the highest being, which in deism is merely transcendent, his objections are very strong, and according to how this concept is arranged, in certain cases (in fact in all usual cases) irrefutable. HUME always holds on to this: that through the mere concept of an original being, to which we attribute none other than ontological predicates (eternity, omnipresence, omnipotence), we really think nothing determinate, and properties would have to be added which can yield a concept *in concreto*; it is not enough to say: he is cause, but rather what his causality is like, perhaps through understanding or will. That is where his attack meets the thing itself, namely theism; previously he had only assaulted the grounds of proof of deism, which is not a specially threatening thing to do. His dangerous arguments refer without exception to anthropomorphism, which he holds to be inseparable from theism and to make it self-contradictory; but if it were left out theism would also fall with it and there would be nothing but deism left over, out of which one can make nothing, which is useful for nothing, and cannot serve as any foundation of religion and morals. If this inevitability of anthropomorphism were certain, the proofs of the existence of a highest being could be what you will and all be granted, yet we should never be able to determine the concept of this being without involving ourselves in contradictions.

But if we connect the prohibition to avoid all transcendent judgements of pure reason with the apparently contradictory command to proceed to concepts which lie outside the field of immanent (empirical) use, we become aware that both can subsist together, but only exactly on the *boundary* of all permitted use of reason ; for the boundary belongs both to the field of experience and to that of the beings of thought. At the same time we learn how those remarkable ideas serve solely to determine the boundaries of human reason, namely on the one hand not to extend knowledge by experience without bounds, so that nothing is left for us to know but merely world, and on the other hand not to go beyond the boundary of experience and try to make judgements about things outside it as things in themselves.

We keep to this boundary if we limit our judgement merely to the relation which the world may have to a being, the concept of which itself lies outside all knowledge of which we are capable inside the world. For we then attribute to the highest being *in itself* none of the properties through which we think objects of experience, and thereby avoid *dogmatic* anthropomorphism ; but we attribute these properties to the relation of this being to the world, and allow ourselves a *symbolic* anthropomorphism, which in fact only concerns language and not the object.

When I say, we are compelled to regard the world *as if* it were the work of a highest understanding and will, I am really saying nothing more than : as a clock, a ship, a regiment is related to the artisan, architect, commander, so the world of the senses (or everything that constitutes the foundation of this totality of appearances) is related to the unknown. By this, though I do not know it for what it is in itself, I know it for what it is for me, namely in respect of the world of which I am a part.

§ 58

Such knowledge is knowledge *by analogy*, which means not, as the word is commonly taken, an imperfect similarity of two things, but a perfect similarity of two relations between quite dissimilar things.* By means of this analogy we are left with a concept of the highest being adequately determined *for us*, although we have left out everything that could *determine* it absolutely and *in itself*; for we determine it in respect of the world and of us, and we need no more. The attacks which HUME made on those who want to determine this concept absolutely, by taking materials for it from themselves and the world, do not touch us ; and he cannot reproach us that we should have nothing left over if the objective anthropomorphism were taken away from our concept of the highest being.

If we are once granted at the start (as HUME in the person of Philo[1] does to Cleanthes in his Dialogues) as a necessary hypothesis the *deistic* concept of the original being, in which the original being is thought through nothing but ontological predicates of substance, cause, etc., (*which we*

---

* Thus there is an analogy between the legal relation of human acts and the mechanical relation of moving forces. I can never do anything to anybody without giving him the right to do the same to me under the same conditions ; likewise no body can act on another with its motive force without causing the other to act reciprocally by the same amount. Right and motive force are quite dissimilar things, but in their relation there is complete similarity. Hence by means of such an analogy I can give a relational concept of things that are absolutely unknown to me. For example as promotion of the happiness of children = a is related to parental love = b, so the well-being of the human species = c is related to the unknown in God = x, which we call love ; not as if it had the least similarity with any human inclination, but because we can posit its relation to the world as similar to that which things in the world have among themselves. But the relational concept here is a mere category, namely the concept of cause, which has nothing to do with sensibility.

---

[1] Some recent commentators have held that Hume is to be identified not with Philo but with Cleanthes.

must do, because reason, impelled by nothing but conditions which are in their turn conditioned, can have no satisfaction in the world of the senses unless we do this, and *which we can fittingly do* without involving ourselves in anthropomorphism and transferring predicates from the world of the senses to a being quite different from the world, because these predicates are mere categories which indeed give no determinate concept of this being, but also no concept limited to the conditions of sensibility) ; then nothing can prevent us from predicating of this being a *causality through reason* in respect of the world, and thus going over to theism, but without being compelled to attribute this reason to the being in itself as a property attached to it.   For as concerns the *first*,[1] the only possible way to force the use of reason, in respect of all possible experience in the world of the senses, to its highest degree thoroughly consistently with itself, is to assume a highest reason as cause in its turn of all the connections in the world ; such a principle is bound to be thoroughly advantageous to reason, and cannot harm it anywhere in its natural use.   *Secondly*[2] on the other hand reason is not thereby transferred as a property to the original being in itself, but only *to the relation* of this being to the world of the senses, and thus anthropomorphism is wholly avoided.   For here only the *cause* of the rational form which is found on all sides in the world is being considered, and reason is indeed being attributed to the highest being, in that it contains the ground of this rational form in the world, but only by analogy, i.e. in that this term only indicates the relation that the highest cause which is unknown to us has to the world, in order to determine everything in the world in the highest degree of conformity with reason.   We thereby avoid using the property of reason in order to think God, but only use it to think the world by means of it in such a way as is necessary in order to have the greatest possible use of

[1] Refers to " *which we must do* ", above.
[2] Refers to " *which we can fittingly do* ".

reason in respect of the world according to a principle. We thereby admit : that the highest being is wholly inscrutable for us as to what it is in itself and even unthinkable *in a determinate way*, and are thereby prevented from making a transcendent use of the concepts of reason which we have, namely our concepts of reason as an efficient cause (by means of the will), in order to determine the divine nature according to these concepts by properties which are always only taken from human nature, and lose ourselves in crude and fatuous concepts. On the other hand we are prevented from flooding our observation of the world with hyperphysical kinds of explanation, according to our concepts of human reason transferred to God, and from deflecting it from its proper destiny, according to which it should be a study of mere nature by reason, and not a foolhardy deduction of its appearances from a highest reason. The expression appropriate to our weak concepts will be : that we think the world *as if* it stemmed from a highest reason as to its existence and its inner determination. For the one part we recognise thereby the quality that is attributable to the world itself and do not presume to determine that of its cause in itself ; for the other part we place the ground of this quality (the rational form of the world) *in the relation* of the highest cause to the world, and do not find the world sufficient by itself for this form.*

Thus the difficulties which seem to stand in the way of theism disappear, in that we join to HUME's principle not to force the use of reason dogmatically outside the field of all possible experience a second principle which HUME

* I shall say : the causality of the highest cause is that in respect of the world which human reason is in respect of its artefacts. The nature of the highest cause itself remains unknown to me ; I only compare its effect known to me (the order of the world) and the conformity of this to reason with the effects known to me of human reason, and hence call the former a reason, without attributing to it as its property the same that I understand by this term in a man or anything else known to me.

completely overlooked, namely : not to regard the field of
possible experience as that which in the eyes of our reason
sets its own boundaries. Critique of reason indicates here
the true middle way between the dogmatism against which
HUME fought and the scepticism which he wished to introduce in opposition to it—a middle way which, unlike other
middle ways, one is not advised to determine for oneself
as it were mechanically (a little of one and a little of the
other), and through which no-one is any the wiser, but
a middle way that can be determined exactly according
to principles.

§ 59

At the beginning of this note I used the metaphor of a
boundary in order to fix the limits of reason in respect of
its appropriate use. The world of the senses merely contains appearances, which are not yet things in themselves ;
the understanding must assume these latter (noumena)
because it knows the objects of experience for mere appearances. In our reason both are comprised together, and the
question is : how does reason proceed to set bounds to the
understanding in respect of both these fields ? Experience,
which contains everything that belongs to the world of
the senses, does not itself set its own bounds ; from every
conditioned it always reaches only to another conditioned.
Whatever is to be its boundary must lie wholly outside it,
and this is the field of pure beings of the understanding.
But for us this is empty space in so far as it is a question of
the *determination* of the nature of these beings of the understanding, and if dogmatically determined concepts are then
the aim we cannot go outside the field of possible experience.
But as a boundary is itself something positive which belongs
both to what lies inside it and to the space which lies outside
a given totality, reason partakes in real positive knowledge
merely by extending itself up to this boundary, but in such
a way that it does not try to go beyond this boundary,

because it finds there before it an empty space in which it can indeed think forms for things but not things themselves. But yet the *bounding* of the field of experience by something which is otherwise unknown to it is knowledge which remains to reason from this point of view ; in this knowledge reason, neither enclosed inside the world of the senses nor extravagating outside it, limits itself, as is proper to knowledge of a boundary, merely to the relation of that which lies outside the boundary to that which is contained inside it.

Natural theology is such a concept on the boundary of human reason. In it reason finds itself compelled to look out towards the idea of a highest being (and in reference to practice also towards the idea of an intelligible world), not in order to determine anything in respect of this mere being of the understanding outside the world of the senses, but only to direct its own use inside the world of the senses according to principles of the greatest possible (theoretical as well as practical) unity, and on this behalf to make use of the reference of these principles to an independent reason as cause of all these connections. Reason is not however compelled thereby merely to *invent* for itself a being ; but as, outside the world of the senses, there must necessarily be something to be found which only the pure understanding thinks, reason is compelled to *determine* a being in this way, although indeed merely by analogy.

In this way our above proposition, which is the result of the whole critique, can stand : "that reason never teaches us by all its principles *a priori* anything more than solely objects of possible experience, and of these nothing more than what can be known in experience " ; but this limitation does not prevent reason from leading us up to the objective *boundary* of experience, i.e. to the *reference* to something which must not itself be an object of experience but must be the highest ground of all experience, teaching us nothing in itself about this thing but only something in reference to reason's own use, complete and directed to the highest ends, in the field of possible experience. But this is all the utility that we can reasonably wish for, and we have cause to be satisfied with it.

§ 60

We have now exhibited metaphysics completely according to its subjective possibility, as it is really given *in the natural disposition* of human reason, and indeed in what constitutes the essential end of cultivating it. We found nevertheless that this *merely natural* use of this natural disposition of our reason involves reason in transcendent dialectical inferences which are partly merely illusory and partly even self-contradictory, if no discipline which is only possible through a scientific critique bridles it and keeps it in limits ; and we also found that for the promotion of knowledge of nature this sophistical metaphysics can be dispensed with, indeed is detrimental to it. It thus still remains a problem worthy of enquiry to find out the *natural ends* to which this disposition in our reason to transcendent concepts may be aimed, because everything that lies in nature must be originally aimed at some useful end.

Such an enquiry is in fact dangerous : and I admit that what I can say about it is only conjecture, as is everything that concerns the first ends of nature. This may be allowed to me in this case alone, because the question does not concern the objective validity of metaphysical judgements, but the natural disposition to metaphysical judgements, and therefore lies outside the system of metaphysics, in anthropology.

When I [.........[1]] all the transcendental ideas the totality of which constitutes the proper problem of natural pure reason, which compels it to leave mere observation of nature and to go beyond all possible experience, and in this endeavour to bring into being the thing (whether it be knowledge or sophistry) that is called metaphysics, I believe I perceive that this natural disposition is aimed at freeing

---

[1] This sentence is grammatically defective in the original editions and contains no verb.

our comprehension from the fetters of experience and the limits of mere observation of nature far enough for it at least to see opened before it a field that merely contains objects for the pure understanding which no sensibility can reach ; not indeed with the intention that we should occupy ourselves with it speculatively (because we find no ground on which we can get a foot-hold), but in order that practical principles, which unless they found before them such a space for their necessary expectation and hope, would not be able to extend themselves to that universality which reason absolutely must have for moral purposes, [......[1]]

Now I find that the *psychological* idea, however little insight it gives me into the pure nature of the human soul elevated above all concepts of experience, does at least show clearly enough the inadequacy of the latter and diverts me from materialism as a psychological concept fit for no explanation of nature and in addition in a practical regard restrictive of reason. Similarly the *cosmological* ideas, through the visible inadequacy of all possible knowledge of nature to satisfy reason in its legitimate enquiries, serve to keep us away from naturalism, which gives out that nature is sufficient in itself. Finally, all natural necessity in the world of the senses always being conditioned, in that it always presupposes the dependence of things on other things, whereas unconditioned necessity must be sought only in the unity of a cause different from the world of the senses ; and the causality of natural necessity in its turn, if it were merely nature, never being able to make conceivable the existence of the contingent as its consequence : reason thus rids itself, by means of the *theological* idea, of fatalism, both the fatalism of a blind natural necessity in the system of nature itself without a first principle and the fatalism in the causality of this principle itself, and leads to the concept of a cause through freedom and hence of a highest intelligence. Thus the transcendental ideas serve, if not to teach us

---

[1] This sentence is also incomplete.

positively, yet to cancel the impudent assertions of *material-ism*, *naturalism* and *fatalism*, which restrict the field of reason, and thereby to make room for moral ideas outside the field of speculation ; and this it seems to me would explain in some degree this natural disposition.

The practical utility which a merely speculative science may have lies outside the boundaries of this science ; it can thus be regarded merely as a scholium, and like all scholia does not belong to the science itself as a part of it. None the less this reference does at least lie inside the boundaries of philosophy, especially of that philosophy which draws from the pure sources of reason, where the speculative use of reason in metaphysics must necessarily have unity with the practical use of reason in ethics. Hence the inevitable dialectic of pure reason in a metaphysics, regarded as a natural disposition, deserves to be explained not merely as an illusion that needs to be resolved, but also as a *natural institution* according to its end ; although this job being supererogatory cannot rightly be expected of metaphysics proper.

A second scholium more closely related to the content of metaphysics would be the solution of the questions on pages 647–668 [1] of the Critique. Certain principles of reason [2] are there expounded which determine *a priori* the order of nature, or rather determine the understanding which must seek the laws of nature through experience. They seem to be constitutive and legislative in respect of experience though they originate from mere reason which must not be regarded, like the understanding, as a principle

---

[1] i.e. A647–668/B675–696. The section : " Appendix to the transcendental Dialectic : Of the regulative use of the Ideas of Pure Reason " ends at A668 but begins at A642, for which the reference given could be a mistake.

[2] These are the principles of (i) the homogeneity of the manifold under higher genera ; (ii) the variety of the homogeneous under lower species ; (iii) the affinity of (continuous transition between) all concepts (A657/B685).

of possible experience. Those who want to track down the nature of reason outside its use in metaphysics, in the universal principles for making systematic a natural history in general, may consider further whether this agreement rests on this : that just as nature is not attached to appearances or their source, sensibility, in themselves, but is only found in the reference of appearances to the understanding, likewise the thoroughgoing unity of the use of the understanding on behalf of a total possible experience (in a system) can only be attributed to the understanding with reference to reason, and thus experience also stands indirectly under the legislature of reason. In the work itself I have represented this problem as important, but I have not attempted its solution.*

And thus I conclude the analytical solution of the main question I set up myself : how is metaphysics in general possible ? by ascending from where its use is really given, at least in its consequences, to the grounds of its possibility.

---

* It was my continuous intention throughout the Critique not to omit anything which could bring the enquiry into the nature of pure reason to completion, however deeply it might lie hidden. It is afterwards open to everyone's choice how far he wants to take his enquiry if only he has been shown what enquiries might still be undertaken ; for this can fairly be expected of him who has made it his business to survey this whole field, so as to leave it afterwards to others for future cultivation and allotment according to choice. To this belong the two scholia which because of their dryness would hardly recommend themselves to amateurs, and hence have only been put forward for experts.

Metaphysics as a natural disposition of reason is real, but by itself (as the analytical solution to the third main question proved) it is dialectical and deceptive. To try to draw principles from this natural disposition and to follow in their use this natural but none the less false illusion can never produce science but only vain dialectical art, in which one school can outdo another but none can ever earn rightful and lasting esteem.

For metaphysics to be able, as a science, to claim not merely deceptive persuasion but insight and conviction, a critique of reason itself must exhibit the whole stock of concepts *a priori*, the division of them according to their different sources, sensibility, understanding and reason, further a complete table of them and the analysis of all these concepts with everything that can be inferred from them ; further and especially, a critique must exhibit the possibility of synthetic knowledge *a priori* by means of a deduction of these concepts, the principles of their use and finally also the boundaries of their use ; and everything must be in a complete system. Thus a critique, and only a critique, contains in itself the whole well-tested and proved plan, and indeed all the means to carry it out, according to which metaphysics as a science can be brought into being ; by other ways and means it is impossible. Thus the question here is not how this job is possible, but only how it can be got under way and how good brains can be shifted from their present mistaken and fruitless treatment of the matter to an undeceptive treatment, and how such an association could be most fittingly directed to the common end.

So much is certain : whoever has once tasted criticism will always be nauseated by all dogmatic drivel which he had to be satisfied with before of necessity, because his reason needed something and could find nothing better for its sustenance. Criticism is related to ordinary school-metaphysics exactly as *chemistry* to *alchemy*, or as *astronomy* to the divinations of *astrology*. I guarantee that nobody who has thought through and grasped the principles of criticism even only in these prolegomena will ever return again to that old and sophistical mock-science ; rather will he look forward with a certain delight to a metaphysics which is now surely in his power, which needs no more preparatory discoveries, and which for the first time can provide reason with lasting satisfaction. For that is the advantage on which metaphysics alone among all possible sciences can count with confidence, i.e. that it can be brought to completion and to a permanent state in which it may not be changed further and is capable of no increase through new discoveries ; because reason has here the sources of its knowledge not in objects and their intuition (through which it can be taught nothing more), but in itself, and when it has exhibited the fundamental laws of its faculty complete and determined to the exclusion of all misinterpretation, nothing remains that pure reason could know *a priori*, indeed nothing that it could have ground for asking. The sure prospect of a knowledge so determinate and closed has a particular attraction, even if all the utility (of which I shall say more hereafter) is put aside.

All false art, all vain wisdom lasts its time out, then in the end it destroys itself and the highest cultivation of it is at the same time the point of its decline. That this time has now arrived in respect of metaphysics is proved by the state into which it has fallen among all learned peoples, considering all the zeal with which other sciences of all kinds are being pursued. The old ordinance of university studies still keeps up the shadow of metaphysics, a solitary academy of sciences from time to time moves one or the

other by offering prizes to make an essay in it, but it is
no longer counted among sound sciences and one may judge
for oneself how a learned man would take this well-meant
praise envied by almost no-one, if one were to call him a
great metaphysician.

But although the time of the fall of all dogmatic metaphysics has undoubtedly arrived, much is still lacking for
one to be able to say on the other hand that the time of
its re-birth by means of a sound and complete critique
of reason has already appeared. All transitions from one
inclination to the opposite go through the state of indifference, and this point of time is the most dangerous for an
author but, as it seems to me, the most favourable for the
science. For if through the complete breaking of previous
connections the party spirit has died out, minds are in the
best condition for gradually beginning to listen to proposals
for connections according to a different plan.

When I say that I hope that these prolegomena will
perhaps promote lively enquiry in the field of criticism, and
will offer to the universal spirit of philosophy, which seems
to lack nourishment in the speculative part, a new and
promising object of sustenance, I can imagine to myself in
advance that everyone who has been made unwilling and
weary by the thorny paths through which I have led him
in the critique will ask me, on what do I ground this hope?
I reply, *on the irresistible law of necessity.*

It is as little to be expected that the spirit of man will one
day wholly give up metaphysical enquiries, as that in order
not to be always breathing impure air we shall one day
prefer to give up breathing altogether. There will always
be metaphysics in the world, and what is more in everyone,
especially in every thinking man; but in the absence of a
public standard everyone will cut his metaphysics in his
own way. What has hitherto been called metaphysics can
satisfy no enquiring brain, but wholly to renounce metaphysics is also impossible. Thus a critique of pure reason
itself must in the end be *attempted*, or if one exists *examined*

and submitted to general testing, because there is no other means of satisfying this present need which is something more than mere curiosity.

Since I have known criticism I have never been able to prevent myself from asking, when I have read a work of metaphysical content which has both entertained and educated me by the determination of its concepts, by variety and order and an easy exposition : *has this author taken metaphysics one step further ?* I ask the learned men for pardon, whose writings have been useful to me from other points of view and have always contributed to the cultivation of the powers of the mind, for admitting that neither in their nor in my own lesser essays (which vanity enhances) have I been able to find that the science has been taken the least step further by them, and this from the quite natural ground that the science did not yet exist and cannot be put together bit by bit but must have its seed fully pre-formed in the critique. To avoid all misinterpretation one must remember from above that analytical treatment of our concepts is indeed of great utility to the understanding, but that the science (of metaphysics) is not thereby taken the least step further, because these analyses of concepts are only materials out of which the science has yet to be constructed. An analysis and determination of the concept of substance and accident may be as good as you like ; that is very good preparation for some future use. But if I cannot prove that in everything that exists substance is permanent and only the accidents change, all this analysis has not taken the science the least step further. Now metaphysics has not hitherto been able to prove as *a priori* valid either this proposition or the principle of sufficient reason, much less any more complex principle, such as for example one belonging to psychology or cosmology, and indeed no synthetic proposition at all ; thus all this analysis accomplishes nothing, creates nothing and promotes nothing, and after so much pother and noise the science is still where it was in the time of ARISTOTLE, although the preparations for it, once the clue to synthetic knowledge had been found, are undoubtedly much better arranged than before.

If anyone takes offence at this he can easily nullify this accusation by quoting a single synthetic proposition belonging to metaphysics which he offers to prove *a priori* in a dogmatic way ; for only if he achieves this will I grant that he has really brought the science a step further, even though this proposition were otherwise well enough confirmed by ordinary experience. No demand can be more moderate and fairer, and in the (infallibly certain) case of its not being satisfied, no pronouncement more just than this : that metaphysics as a science has hitherto not existed at all.

In case the challenge is taken up I must decline two things : first, the child's play of *probability* and conjecture which suits metaphysics as badly as it does geometry ; secondly decision by means of the divining rod of so-called *sound common sense* which does not dip for everybody but goes by personal qualities.

For *as far as the first is concerned*, there can be nothing more absurd than to try to ground one's judgements on probability and conjecture in metaphysics which is a philosophy out of pure reason. Everything that is to be known *a priori* is thereby declared to be apodictically certain, and must be proved to be such. One might as well try to ground a geometry or an arithmetic on conjectures ; for as concerns the *calculus probabilium* of the latter, it does not contain probable but quite certain judgements on the degree of possibility of certain cases under given homogeneous conditions, which in the sum of all possible cases must happen quite infallibly according to the rule, although in respect of every particular incident the rule is not sufficiently determined. Only in empirical natural science can conjectures (by means of induction and analogy) be suffered, and only in such a way that at least the possibility of what I assume must be completely certain.

With *the appeal to sound common sense* when [we are concerned with [1]] concepts and principles, not in so far as they are to be valid in respect of experience, but in so far as they are to be declared valid outside the conditions of experience, matters are if possible still worse. For what is *sound sense?* It is common sense [understanding [2]], in so far as it judges correctly. And what is common sense? It is the faculty of knowledge and of the use of rules *in concreto*, in distinction from the *speculative* understanding, which is a faculty of knowledge of rules *in abstracto*. Thus common sense will hardly be able to understand the rule : that everything that happens is determined by means of its cause, and will certainly never be able to have insight into it in general. Hence it demands an example from experience, and when it hears that this means nothing else than what it has always thought when a window-pane was broken or something was lost about the house, it understands the principle and grants it. Common sense thus has no further use than in so far as it can see its rules confirmed in experience (although the rules are really present in it *a priori*) ; to have insight into them *a priori* and independently of experience belongs to the speculative understanding, and lies quite outside the field of vision of common sense. Metaphysics has to do solely with the latter kind of knowledge, and it is certainly a bad sign of sound sense to appeal to that surety, who has no judgement here and at whom one otherwise only looks down one's nose, except when one is in trouble and does not know where to look for advice or help in one's speculations.

It is an ordinary subterfuge which these false friends of common sense (who occasionally value it highly but com-

---

[1] Text defective ; this or some similar phrase must be supplied.

[2] The word translated by " sense " in this paragraph is the word (" *Verstand* ") which is elsewhere translated " understanding ". The apposition of common sense (*Verstand*) and speculative understanding (*Verstand*) cannot be reproduced. Similar difficulties were noted on page 9.

monly despise it) are in the habit of using, to say: there
must in the end be some propositions which are immediately
certain and of which not only no proof but no justification
at all need be given, because otherwise there would be no
end to the grounds of one's judgements.   To prove their
right to say this, the only indisputable things they can ever
quote (except for the principle of contradiction, which is
not competent to show the truth of synthetic propositions)
which they can attribute immediately to common sense,
are mathematical propositions : e.g. that twice two makes
four, that there is only one straight line between two points,
etc.   But these are judgements which are worlds apart from
those of metaphysics.   For in mathematics I myself can
make through my thought (construct) everything that I
represent to myself as possible through a concept ; to the
one two I add gradually another two and myself make the
figure four, or I draw all kinds of lines in thought from one
point to the other and can only see one which is similar to
itself in all its parts (equal as well as unequal).   But with
the whole power of my thought I cannot bring forth from
the concept of one thing the concept of another thing the
existence of which is necessarily connected with the first, but
I must take counsel of experience.   Although my understanding provides me *a priori* (but always only in reference
to possible experience) with the concept of such a connection
(of causality), I cannot exhibit it *a priori* in intuition, like the
concepts of mathematics, and thus show its possibility *a
priori* ; this concept together with the principles of its
application always needs, if it is to be valid *a priori*—as
is demanded in metaphysics—a justification and deduction
of its possibility, because otherwise one will not know how
far it is valid and whether it can be used only in experience
or also outside it.   Thus there can be no appeal in metaphysics as a speculative science of pure reason to common
sense ; but there can well be such an appeal when (in
certain matters) we are compelled to leave metaphysics and
to renounce all pure speculative knowledge (which must

always be a knowing) including metaphysics itself and its teaching, and when rational belief alone is found possible for us and adequate for our need (and even perhaps more wholesome than this knowing itself). For then the shape of the thing is quite altered. Metaphysics must be science, not only as a whole but in all its parts, otherwise it is nothing at all ; because as speculation of pure reason it has no other support than from universal insights. Outside metaphysics probability and common sense can well have their useful and legitimate employment, but according to principles of their own, the importance of which always depends on their reference to the practical.

That is what I hold myself justified in demanding for the possibility of metaphysics as a science.

OF WHAT CAN BE DONE TO MAKE
METAPHYSICS AS A SCIENCE
REAL

As all the paths that have hitherto been taken have not reached this end, and as this end never will be reached without a preceding critique of pure reason, it seems not unfair to expect that the essay in it which is here presented should be submitted to an exact and careful examination, unless anyone holds it more advisable rather to give up all claims to metaphysics completely, in which case, if he remains true to his resolution, there is nothing to be said against it. But if one takes the course of affairs as they really are and not as they ought to be, there are two kinds of judgements, a *judgement which precedes enquiry,* and such is in our case that in which the reader passes a judgement on the critique of pure reason from his metaphysics (the possibility of which the critique has yet to examine) ; and then a different *judgement which follows enquiry,* in which the reader is able to put on one side for a time the consequences of the critical enquiries, which may offend rather strongly against his previously accepted metaphysics, and first tests the grounds from which these consequences may be deduced. If that which common metaphysics expounds were established as certain (like geometry), the first kind of judgement would be valid ; for if the consequences of certain principles conflict with established truths, those principles are false, and are to be rejected without any further enquiry. But if it is the case that metaphysics does not have a stock of indisputably certain (synthetic) propositions, even perhaps that many which are as plausible as the best among them, are none the less in conflict among themselves in their consequences, and that no sure criterion whatever of the truth of properly metaphysical (synthetic) propositions is to be found in metaphysics at all : then the first kind of judgement can have no place, and an examination of the principles of the critique must precede any judgement about its value.

Specimen
of a Judgement on the Critique which precedes enquiry

Such a judgement is to be found in the Göttingische gelehrte Anzeigen, third part of the supplement, of 19th January 1782, page 40 et seq.[1]

If an author who is well acquainted with the object of his work, who has been sedulous to put what is entirely his own reflection into the treatment of it, falls into the hands of a reviewer who for his part is perspicacious enough to spy out the moments on which the value or absence of it in the work properly rests, does not hang on words but goes after the matter, and merely sifts and tests the principles from which the author started, then the latter may dislike the severity of the judgement, but the public is indifferent to it, for it is the gainer ; and the author himself can be satisfied at having an opportunity to correct or clarify his essays after they have been tested early by an expert, and in this way, if he believes that at bottom he is in the right, to remove betimes the stumbling-block which could be disadvantageous to his work in the sequel.

With my reviewer I find myself in quite a different situation. He seems to have no insight into what was properly at issue in the enquiry with which (happily or unhappily) I occupied myself, and whether it is the fault of impatience to think through a prolix work, or bad temper over a threatened reform of a science in which he

---

[1] This review was contributed by Christian Garve and very severely cut in its length by the editor, J. G. Feder. A correspondence between Garve and Kant ensued, in which Garve took advantage of this circumstance to disclaim responsibility for the tenor of the review as printed—a disclaimer which was seen to have little foundation when Garve's review was published again in full in the periodical *Allgemeine Deutsche Bibliothek* in 1783 (p. 838).

believed he had cleared up everything long ago, or, which I am loath to suppose, a really limited comprehension which prevents him from ever thinking himself beyond his school-metaphysics—in short, he hurries impetuously through a long list of propositions with which one can think nothing at all without knowing their premises, now and again scatters his censure, of which the reader sees the ground as little as he understands the propositions against which it is supposed to be directed, and thus can neither be useful to the public for information nor do me the least damage in the judgement of the experts.   Hence I would have completely ignored this judgement if it did not give me the occasion for some clarifications which might in some cases save the reader of these Prolegomena from misinterpretations.

In order that the reviewer may take up a point of view from which he can most easily present the whole work in a way unfavourable to the author, without needing to trouble himself with any particular enquiry, he begins and ends by saying : " this work is a system of transcendent [1] (or, as he translates it, of higher) * idealism ".

As soon as I caught sight of these lines I saw what sort of a review would emerge.   Much as if someone who had

* Not on your life the *higher*.   High towers, and metaphysically tall men like them, round both of which there is commonly a lot of wind, are not for me.   My place is the fruitful *bathos* of experience, and the word transcendental, the meaning of which I have indicated so many times though the reviewer has not grasped it once (so cursorily has he looked at everything), does not mean something that goes beyond all experience, but something which, though it precedes (*a priori*) all experience, is not destined for anything more than solely to make knowledge by experience possible.   If these concepts step beyond experience, their use is called transcendent, in distinction from the immanent use, i.e. use limited to experience.   All misinterpretations of this kind are adequately guarded against in the work ; but the reviewer found his advantage in misinterpretations.

[1] The review actually reads " transcendental ", though it uses the form " transcendent*eller* Idealismus " whereas Kant always writes " transcendent*aler* Idealismus ".

never seen or heard anything of geometry were to find a Euclid, and, being requested to give his opinion on it, were to say, after he had come upon a lot of figures on turning over the pages : " The book is a systematic instruction in drawing : the author uses a special language in order to give obscure, unintelligible precepts which are able to achieve nothing more in the end than what anybody could bring about by means of a good eye, etc."

However let us look what sort of an idealism this is that permeates my whole work, although it does not by a long way constitute the soul of the system.

The proposition of all genuine idealists from the ELEATIC SCHOOL to Bishop BERKELEY is contained in this formula : " all knowledge through the senses and through experience is nothing but illusion, and only in the ideas of pure understanding and reason is truth ".

The principle that governs and determines my idealism throughout is on the contrary : " All knowledge of things out of mere pure understanding or pure reason is nothing but illusion, and only in experience is truth."

This is exactly the opposite of that idealism proper ; how then did I come to use this term for a quite opposite purpose, and how did the reviewer come to see it on all sides ?

The solution of this difficulty rests on something that could very easily have been evident, if he had wanted it to be, from the context of the work. Space and time, together with everything that they contain, are not things or their properties in themselves, but merely belong to appearances of them ; and so far I am of one confession with these idealists. But they and among them especially BERKELEY regarded space as a mere empirical representation which, like the appearances in it, only becomes known to us, together with all its determinations, by means of experience or perception ; I on the contrary first show that space (and likewise time, to which BERKELEY paid no attention) with all its determinations can be known by us *a priori* because it, as well as time, is present in us before all perception or experience as pure form of our sensibility, and makes possible all intuition of sensibility, and hence all appearances.   From this it follows : that as truth rests on universal and necessary laws as its criteria, experience with BERKELEY can have no criteria of truth because nothing was laid (by him) *a priori* at the ground of appearances in it, from which it then followed that they are nothing but illusion ; whereas for us space and time (in conjunction with the pure concepts of the understanding) prescribe their law *a priori* to all possible experience, and this yields at the same time the sure criterion for distinguishing truth in it from illusion.*

My so-called (properly critical) idealism is thus of a quite peculiar kind, namely in that it reverses the usual idealism, and through my idealism all knowledge *a priori*, even that of geometry, first receives objective reality, which could not be asserted even by the most zealous realist without this my proved ideality of space and time.   In these circumstances I should like to be able to give my concept a different name, in order to avoid all misunderstanding ; but completely to change it cannot very well be done.   I may therefore be allowed to call it in future, as has already been indicated above,[1] formal or still better critical idealism, in order to distinguish it from the dogmatic idealism of BERKELEY and the sceptical idealism of DESCARTES.

I find nothing further remarkable in the criticism of this

---

* Idealism proper always has a visionary purpose, and can have no other, but my idealism is solely for conceiving the possibility of our knowledge *a priori* of the objects of experience, which is a problem that has not hitherto been solved, or even raised.   Thereby falls the whole visionary idealism, which always (as can already be seen from PLATO) inferred from our knowledge *a priori* (even that of geometry) another intuition than that of the senses (namely intellectual intuition), because it never occurred to anyone that the senses should also intuit *a priori*.

[1] In Note III to the Main transcendental question, first part (p. 46), especially pp. 50-1.

book. The author of it judges through and through *en gros*, a manner which is cleverly chosen because one does not betray in it one's own knowledge or ignorance ; a single full judgement *en détail* would have disclosed, if as is proper it had concerned the main question, perhaps my error, perhaps also the measure of the reviewer's insight in this kind of enquiry. It was a trick not at all badly thought out for taking away in good time from readers accustomed to giving themselves an idea of books out of newspaper reports alone the desire to read the book itself, to reel off one after the other in one breath a lot of propositions which, torn out of the context of their grounds of proof and explanations (especially as antipodic as these are in respect of all school-metaphysics), must necessarily sound nonsensical, to assault the patience of the reader until he is nauseated, and then, after giving oneself away with the significant proposition that constant illusion is truth, to finish with the crude but fatherly lesson : why the quarrel with ordinary language, why and whence the idealistic distinction ? A judgement which, after first declaring it to be metaphysically heretical, in the end makes everything that is peculiar to my book into a mere change of language, and clearly proves that my would-be judge has not in the least understood it and furthermore not understood himself properly.*

But the reviewer speaks like a man who must be aware

---

* The reviewer is in several cases fighting his own shadow. When I oppose the truth of experience to dreams, he never thinks that it is only a question here of the well-known *somnium objective sumtum* [1] of the Wolffian philosophy, which is merely formal, and is not concerned with the difference between sleeping and waking, which has no place in a transcendental philosophy. Incidentally, he calls my deduction of the categories and the table of the principles of the understanding " commonly known principles of logic and ontology expressed in an idealistic way ". On this the reader need only refer to these prolegomena to convince himself that a more miserable and even historically false judgement could not be passed.

[1] " dreams taken objectively "—Wolff's *German Metaphysics*, § 142.

of having important and excellent insights, which however he keeps hidden ; for in respect of metaphysics nothing has recently come to my knowledge which could justify such a tone. He is doing a great wrong in keeping his discoveries from the world ; for there are doubtless others who like myself cannot find that with all the fine things that have been written in this subject for a long time the science has been taken one finger-breadth further. For the rest, sharpening definitions, providing lame proofs with new crutches, giving the patch-work of metaphysics new rags or a different pattern—we find all that, but that is not what the world is asking for. The world has had enough of metaphysical assertions ; what is wanted is an enquiry into the possibility of this science and the sources from which certainty in it could be deduced, and to have sure criteria for distinguishing the dialectical illusion of pure reason from truth. The reviewer must possess the key to this, otherwise he would never have spoken in so high a tone.

But I come to suspect that this need of the science may perhaps never have entered his thoughts, for otherwise he would have directed his judgement to this point, and in so important a matter even an attempt which had miscarried would have won his esteem. If that is so, we are good friends again. He may think himself as deep into his metaphysics as he likes, no-one should hinder him, but he cannot judge about that which lies outside metaphysics, the source of it in reason. That my suspicion is not without ground I prove by the fact that he does not say a single word about the possibility of synthetic knowledge *a priori*, which was properly the problem on the solution of which the fate of metaphysics wholly rests and to which my Critique (as here my Prolegomena) was entirely directed. The idealism which he struck and to which he stuck was only taken up into the system as the sole means of solving that problem, (although it then also received confirmation from other grounds), and he would have had to show either that the problem does not have the importance which I give to it (as also in the Prolegomena), or that it has not been solved by my concept of appearances, or could be solved in a better way; but I find no word of this in the review. The reviewer thus understood nothing of my work, and perhaps also nothing of the spirit and essence of metaphysics itself, unless, as I prefer to assume, a reviewer's haste, enraged by the difficulty of working through so many obstacles, threw an unfavourable shadow over the work before him and made it unknowable to him in its fundamental features.

A great deal is still required for a learned journal, however carefully selected and well-chosen its contributors, to be able to establish in the field of metaphysics as elsewhere its otherwise merited reputation. Other sciences and branches of knowledge have their standard. Mathematics has its standard in itself, history and theology in secular or sacred books, natural science and medicine in mathematics and experience, jurisprudence in law books, and even matters of taste in ancient models. But for judging the thing called metaphysics, the standard has yet to be found (I have made an attempt to determine it and its use). What is to be done, until this standard has been worked out, when writings of this kind have to be judged? If they are of the dogmatic kind, let people do as they like; no-one will be able to play the master for long over another, before someone is found to make things equal again. But if they are of the critical kind, and critical not of other writings but of reason itself, so that the standard of judgement cannot be assumed but must first be sought, then let objection and censure be admitted, but on a ground of tolerance, because the need is common and the lack of the needed insight makes a show as of a decision at law out of place.

But in order at the same time to connect this my defence with the interest of the philosophising public, I propose an experiment which will decide about the way in which all metaphysical enquiries are to be directed to their common end. This is nothing other than what mathematicians have done elsewhere to settle a dispute about the superiority of their methods, namely a challenge to my reviewer to prove in his own way any single truly metaphysical principle asserted by him, i.e. synthetic and known *a priori* from concepts, and possibly one of the most indispensable, e.g. the principle of the permanence of substance, or of the necessary determination of events in the world by a cause, but as is proper from grounds *a priori*. If he cannot do this (silence is confession) he must grant : that as metaphysics is nothing whatever without the apodictical certainty of propositions of this kind, the possibility or impossibility of it must before all else first be settled in a critique of pure reason, and he is bound either to admit that my principles of criticism are correct, or to prove their invalidity. But as I already foresee that however carefree his reliance on the certainty of his principles may hitherto have been, yet when it is a question of a strict test, he will not be able to find a single principle in the whole extent of metaphysics with which he can boldly appear, I will allow him the most favorable condition which one can expect in a competition, namely take the *onus probandi* from him and let it be placed on me.

He finds in these Prolegomena and in my Critique pp. 426–461 [1] eight propositions which conflict with each other pair by pair, of which every one belongs necessarily to metaphysics which must either accept or refute it (although there is not one which has not been accepted at some time by some philosopher). Now he has the freedom to choose one of these eight propositions at his pleasure, to accept it without proof, which I allow him, but only one (for the waste of time will serve him as little as it serves me), and then attack my proof of the contrary. If I can still rescue this proposition and show in this way that according to principles which every dogmatic metaphysics must necessarily recognise, the contrary of the proposition he has adopted can be proved equally clearly, then it is established that there is a hereditary fault in metaphysics

[1] i.e. A426–461/B454–489, The Antinomy of Pure Reason.

which cannot be explained, much less removed except by ascending to its birthplace, pure reason itself. Thus my Critique must either be accepted, or a better one put in its place, and mine therefore at least studied ; which is all that I demand now. If I cannot rescue my proof, a synthetic proposition *a priori* stands firm on dogmatic principles on the side of my opponent, my accusation against ordinary metaphysics was therefore unjust, and I offer to recognise his censure of my Critique as legitimate (although that should not by a long way be the consequence). For this purpose, it seems to me, it would be necessary *to leave the incognito*, as I do not see how it could otherwise be prevented that instead of one problem, I should be honoured or assaulted with several by unknown and uncalled opponents.

Proposal
for an examination of the Critique on which a judgement can follow

I am obliged to the learned public for the silence with which it has honoured my Critique for a considerable time ; for this proves a postponement of judgement and thus some suspicion that in a work which leaves all accustomed paths and sets out on a new one in which one cannot at once find one's way, something may perhaps lie through which an important but at present dead branch of human knowledge may receive new life and fruitfulness, and also a care not to break and destroy the delicate shoot by an overhasty judgement. A specimen of a judgement delayed on such grounds has just come to my sight in the Gothaische gelehrte Zeitung,[1] the soundness of which (without taking into account my suspicious praise) every reader will perceive for himself from the easily comprehensible and unfalsified account of a piece belonging to the first principles of my work.

[1] Of 24th August 1782. Up to this time this was the only review of the *Critique* other than the Göttingen review.

And now I propose, as an extensive building cannot possibly be judged at once as a whole by a cursory estimate, that it should be tested, piece by piece, from its foundations up, and that these Prolegomena should be used as a general sketch, with which the work itself could be compared as convenient. This suggestion, if it were based on nothing more than the imagined importance which vanity ordinarily lends to all products of one's own, would be immodest and would deserve to be rejected with displeasure. But the affairs of speculative philosophy as a whole are such that they are on the point of being wholly extinguished, although human reason holds on to them with an undying affection which is trying, although vainly, to turn itself into indifference, only because it is ceaselessly disappointed.

In our thinking age it is not to be supposed that many deserving men should not use every good occasion to work together in the common interest of a reason which is growing ever more enlightened, if only there is some hope of thereby reaching the goal. Mathematics, natural science, laws, arts, even ethics etc., do not completely fill the soul ; there is always space left in it which is marked out for this merely pure and speculative reason, the emptiness of which compels us to seek in grotesques or baubles, or in enthusiasm, a seeming occupation and entertainment, but at bottom only distraction, to drown the burdensome call of reason which in conformity with its destiny demands something that will satisfy it for itself and not merely set it busy to other ends or in the interest of fancies. Hence considerations which occupy themselves merely with this extent of reason subsisting for itself have a great attraction, as I have grounds for supposing, for everyone who has ever tried to enlarge his comprehension in this way, because all other knowledge and even ends must meet in it and unite into a whole—I may well say a greater attraction than any other theoretical knowledge, which one would not lightly exchange for this one.

I propose these Prolegomena as a plan and guide for the

enquiry, and not the work itself, because although I am now still well satisfied with it as concerns the content, order and doctrine, and the care which was applied to every sentence, to weigh and test it exactly, before I wrote it down (for it took years fully to satisfy myself in respect of its sources not merely with the whole but sometimes with a single sentence), yet I am not fully satisfied with the exposition in some sections of the Doctrine of Elements, e.g. the deduction of the concepts of the understanding, or that of the paralogisms o.p.r., because a certain prolixity in them obstructs their clarity, and instead of them one may take what the Prolegomena say here in respect of these sections as the basis of the enquiry.

The Germans are praised in that when constancy and sustained diligence are demanded they can go further than other peoples. If this opinion has ground, here is now an opportunity to bring to completion (which has not yet been done successfully) an undertaking the happy outcome of which can hardly be in doubt and in which all thinking men are equally concerned, and to confirm that favorable opinion ; especially as the science which it concerns is of such a special kind that it can be brought once and for all to its whole completeness and into a *permanent state*, in which it cannot be taken the least step further and can be increased by no later discovery, nor even changed (I do not count decoration by greater clarity here and there or added utility for all sorts of purposes) ; an advantage which no other science has or can have, because none concerns a faculty of knowledge so completely isolated, independent of others and unmixed with them. The present moment seems not unfavorable to this my request, as one hardly knows in Germany what, outside the so-called useful sciences, one could occupy oneself with which would not be a mere game, but at the same time an occupation through which a lasting end is achieved.

How the endeavours of scholars could be united to such an end I must leave to others to think out the means. In the meantime it is not my intention to expect of anyone a mere following of my theses, or even to flatter myself with the hope of this, but however attacks, rehearsals, qualifications, or confirmation, completion and extension may contribute to it, if the matter is only examined from the ground up, it cannot fail to happen that a body of doctrine, even if it is not mine, should thereby come into being, which can be a legacy to posterity for which it will have cause to be grateful.

What sort of a metaphysics could be expected in consequence of our once being right with the principles of a critique, and how this would not look miserable and cut down to a small figure through having its false feathers plucked, but could look richly and decently equipped in another regard, would take too long to show here; but other great services which such a reform would bring with it are immediately obvious. Ordinary metaphysics did something useful in seeking out the elementary concepts of pure understanding, in order to make them clear by analysis and determined by explanations. It was thereby a cultivation of reason, wherever it might choose to turn afterwards; but this was all the good that it did. For it destroyed this its merit again by favouring conceit by reckless assertions, sophistry by subtle escapes and excuses, and shallowness through ease in overcoming the most difficult problems with a little school-learning, which is the more seductive the more it has the choice on the one hand of taking on something of the language of a science, on the other hand of popularity, and thereby to be everything for everybody and in fact nothing at all. Criticism on the contrary gives a standard to our judgement, by which knowledge can be surely distinguished from mock-knowledge, and by being brought to its full execution in metaphysics, provides the foundation for a way of thinking which afterwards exerts its beneficent influence on every other use of reason and first inspires the true philosophical spirit. But the service which it renders to theology in making it independent of the judgement of dogmatic speculation, and thus completely securing it against all attacks of such opponents, is certainly not to be underestimated. For ordinary metaphysics, although it promised theology much advantage, could not afterwards fulfil this promise, and in addition, by calling up speculative dogmatics for its support, had done nothing other than to arm enemies against itself. Enthusism, which cannot appear in an enlightened age unless it hides itself behind a school-metaphysics, under the protection of which it can dare as it were to rage rationally, is driven out by critical philosophy from this its last covert. In addition to all this nothing can be so important for a teacher of metaphysics as to be able to say with universal consent that what he is expounding is now at last *science*, and that real service is rendered thereby to the public.